BLACK

WIVES

MATTER

Romel Duane Moore Sr.

Black Wives Matter

Prayer Changes Things (PCT) Publishing
7551 Kingsport Road
Indianapolis, Indiana 46256

Scripture quotations are from the King James Version of the Bible, unless otherwise noted.

Cover design by Alexa Eliza.

No part of this book may be reproduced in any form without permission in writing from the publisher.

Printed in the United States of America.

Edited by Margaret Rose Mejia.

ISBN: 979-8-9872375-1-9
Imprint: Independently Published

Copyright © 2022 by Romel Duane Moore Sr.
All rights reserved.

The name satan is intentionally not capitalized.

TABLE OF CONTENTS

Dedication . . . . Page 4
Foreword . . . . Page 5
Preface . . . . Page 7

Chapter 1 . . . . Eve . . . . Page 11

Chapter 2 . . . . Answer Key . . . . Page 17

Chapter 3 . . . . Hagar . . . . Page 27

Chapter 4 . . . . Keturah . . . . Page 39

Chapter 5 . . . . Esau's Wives . . . . Page 50

Chapter 6 . . . . Tamar . . . . Page 58

Chapter 7 . . . . Wives of Jacob's Sons . . . . Page 71

Chapter 8 . . . . Asenath . . . . Page 79

Chapter 9 . . . . Zipporah . . . . Page 85

Chapter 10 . . . . Daughter of Putiel . . . . Page 100

Chapter 11 . . . . . . Bathsheba & Makeda . . . . Page 108

Chapter 12 . . . . Mother of Rufus . . . . Page 116

Prayer . . . . Page 126

Footnotes . . . . Page 127

DEDICATION

To the Matriarch of my family, my eldest aunt, Jewel Pugh, whose name accentuates her heart and nature. She is the epitome of all the goodness and honor of the Black biblical women chronicled in this book. Jewel is our rock and constant source of calm and wisdom through every storm.

And to my second oldest aunt, Loretta Jones, who has served God faithfully all of my life.

Thank you!

Foreword

Prepare to be catapulted into the lore of ancient, biblical history…even if history is not your forte, it might be after this revealing, riveting read. Romel Moore does not disappoint, as he sews you into the fabric of the plight of these resilient, first Black wives using their illustrious DNA as the thread to bind the struggles of their plight, into the tapestry of today's relative diaspora of the Black family structure. The powerful, descriptive narrative of these Black alpha wives more than inspires, it places the Black woman back on her true pedestal that she originated from with her crown restored, instilling a greater sense of self-worth for Black women of all ages. I consider this work to be an essential manuscript for the Black man to truly fathom the myriad of roles the Black woman plays in his life, while reintroducing an ultimate truism to the Black man in particular: the darker the woman, the deeper his Hebrew roots. Romel Moore had my adrenaline racing with reference to the fact that the Black woman/wife has been time-stamped and approved by Yehova Himself, in the handpicking of a Black woman to be the ultimate progenitor in birthing the Hebrew tribes! This extraordinary historical analysis is akin to a Hebraic balm in Gilead, as Romel Moore delivers the truth, citing receipts to assist in healing the metaphorical scars that ancient Black wives endured… and in many cases Black wives are still coping with the identical struggles of our ancestors, thus making *BLACK WIVES MATTER* one of Romel Moore's most prevalent, profound, and prompt works yet!

Black Wives Matter

Sonya Marie Bowman, Business Owner
Manifest Management Property Enterprises & Royal Herbs Conglomerate
Master's Degree from Concordia University-Mequon & Wisconsin Business Administration
Center of Excellence University

Preface

I'd like to begin by stating I will be referring to Father God and His Son, Jesus, by their Hebrew Names throughout this work. Our English translations of the Bible have lost much of the Essence of Who Father is and through generic references to His Divinity, like referring to Him as simply God, LORD, or Lord, we have failed to know and use His Names and Titles. In the King James Version of the Bible, God is used 2,346 times. LORD (all uppercase letters) is used 6,543 times, and Lord is mentioned 431 times. *LORD* is the Hebrew word *Yehova* or *Yehovah*. The children of Israel considered God's Name so holy and sacred that they only wrote the four consonants of His Name: YHWH. This is called the Tetragrammaton. Over time, vowels were added to YHWH, and they came up with the name *Yahweh*. Because of translations into Greek and English, a "J" was added to *Yehova* or *Yehovah* and the "Y" was dropped which gave us *Jehovah*. This is called transliteration. Transliteration occurs when a word cannot be properly translated into another language, so special efforts are made in attempt to establish a suitable word. A lot of context and meaning are lost in transliterations, and we must recognize this as English-speaking people, especially when it comes to the Names of God.

God is the Hebrew word *Elohim* meaning *Eternal One* or *Self-Existent*. *Lord* is the Hebrew word *Adonay* or *Adonai*. *Adonay* is from an unused root meaning to *rule, sovereign, lord, master,* and *owner*. *Adonay* means *the Lord* (used as a proper Name of God, only). Instead of referring to Father as God, let's get back to calling Him exactly Who He is since we have the privilege of actually knowing His Name or Title. In this writing, I will refer to Daddy as Yahweh, Elohim, Adonai, and Yehovah. We know the name *Jesus* is a Greek and English transliteration from His Hebrew Name *Yeshuah*. Therefore, I will often refer to the Son of God as *Yeshuah* (*Yeshua*). This is purely for educational purposes to become more familiar with the actual Names of God. Whether we use Jesus, Yeshuah, or Yahweh, demons tremble at His Name and must obey when we use it.

Yahweh chose Black women to mother Hebrew bloodlines because mothers are the teachers in the home. He could trust them to raise Hebrew children in His ways and adhere to His commandments. He knew His African queens are deeply spiritual and are His worshippers. A Black woman's discernment and protection for her family is profound and her intercession and assistance to her husband is superior. These are qualities the Most High placed within His Black women for His own purpose. As keepers of their homes, Black wives keep their dwellings impeccable. My grandmother had fifteen children and my aunts and uncles report how immaculate and clean her home was and that you could "eat off the floor." Black women are extraordinary teachers, and nourishers who possess a warrior spirit. The Patriarchs of the Hebrew posterity could not resist these incredible female specimens of strength and beauty. *The Land of Milk and Honey* that Yahweh promised the children of Israel was an African land inhabited by African tribes of Canaan. Yahweh promised to give Israel houses they did not build filled with good things, wells they did not dig, and vineyards and olive trees they did not plant. It was about 470 years from the time Yahweh promised Canaan Land to Abraham and the time the generation of Joshua actually possessed the land. Canaan Land was inhabited by these African descendants of Ham, Noah's son, and remained well-manicured and beautiful for hundreds of years and it is the Black wives who get the credit.

As we witness the deterioration of the Black family in America with sixty-five percent being fatherless, these families are being held together by Divine impartation from Yahweh to his Black mothers and this is Who helps these Black women to stand when all the odds are against her. The first shall be last and the last shall be first. Black women were here first and gave birth to civilizations and her role and importance has returned in these last days to see it all to its end. Before we can speak on Black life, we must first deal with the Black wife, because all life proceeded from her. The term "woke" had its origins in Black activism meaning to "stay awake or aware." It was recently highjacked by White political elitists. "Wokeness" does not invite sensitivity, but it invites controversy. Why is it that men can't be men and women can't be women anymore? A child's gender is assigned by Yahweh. But today the "Woke mob" believes that children can decide which gender they want? The state of Oregon forces their schools to put menstrual products in boys' bathrooms with instructions on how to use them. All nations are sinful, but Divine judgment is inevitable when a nation legalizes the things that Yahweh hates.

Something beautiful happened during the Covid-19 pandemic. During the lockdowns, many wives, and mothers (who were made to not go into work), were at home with their families for an extended time and were able to reconnect with Yahweh's original purpose and joy of being a wife and mother. Some women never returned back to work and others were blessed with the new option of remote employment, working from home. Many companies had to allow their employees to work from the comfort of their homes and this became a perfect fit for untold mothers. Before the pandemic, one out of sixty workers, worked from home. After the pandemic it shifted to one in seven. This was a Godsend because so many mothers were sacrificing mothering in order to make a living.

1

Eve

Mother of All Living

And Adam called his wife's name Eve; because she was the mother of all living.
Genesis 3:20

In the beginning, Elohim created a species in His image and after His likeness and called him "man." The name *Adam* and the word *man* is the same Hebrew word.[1] Before man fell into sin, he was a "living soul" (Genesis 2:7). *Living soul* is the Hebrew words *hay,* and *nepes*.[2] After man fell, we were no longer living souls, but became human beings. Adam and Eve were the only two of Elohim's duplicated creation who were living souls. When Adam and Eve's eyes were opened and they knew they were naked, they had already ceased as living souls and were now looking through the eyes of the flesh as each of us know and appreciate today. We do not know what it is to be living souls and it will never be again. Adam did not name his wife Eve until after they fell. So, what was her name before sin entered in? Her name was the same as the man's name, Adam. Genesis 5:1-2 says:

This is the book of the generations of Adam. In the day that God created man, in the likeness of God made he him;

Male and female created he them; and blessed them, and called their name Adam, in the day when they were created.

Before the Fall, the man and woman were called "Adam." Elohim set the standard for families when the woman takes the name of the man. He created the male to bare the seed thereby possessing the bloodline and since the bloodline comes from the male, the family bears the name of the husband/father. Elohim gave the man the authority to name all living creatures and the man did not give his wife the name "Eve" until after they fell in sin. Genesis 3:20 says, "And Adam called his wife's name Eve; because she was the mother of all living." The enemy is introduced into the affairs of man as "the serpent," and he did not rear his ugly head until after Elohim created the female gender. The serpent waited patiently until Elohim created the opposite sex of male before he made his move, and it was the female gender that he engaged and was able to deceive.

It does not matter how much education, power, or status woman receives in this life, Yahweh was the One who created her and His plan and purpose for her will never change. Woman was made for the man and not the man for her. She is man's helper. We can attempt to change, alter, or even eliminate Yahweh's Divine design for male and female but it will only end in disaster. The female's most valuable asset is her God-given ability to birth life. No accumulation of education, status, power, money, or material assets can trump this. Before a woman runs to be the boss, baller, or conquer the world, Yahweh expects her to fulfill her first Divine purpose that He created her for and that is to be a wife and mother. No one should have more influence in a young child's life than his/her mother. Woman's wisdom, knowledge, love, and creativity is for her children, first. This privilege and honor should not be taken for granted. Having the monetary means to pay for childcare is not as important as caring for your child. She is "the mother of all living," and the day woman believes this power is all but circumstantial, is the day the serpent has beguiled her yet again and her doom is certain. People may call it "archaic," "old-fashioned," and "out-of-date," but Elohim is Creator, and He establishes the purpose for everyone and everything He makes.

Yahweh stated that He would place enmity between the serpent and the woman and the serpent's seed and her seed (Genesis 3:15). We are witnessing the present-day version of this warfare as the terms male and female are under attack. The serpent hates the awesome ability of the woman. She is woman or "womb-man" and her womb will always be the enemy's greatest threat because her womb is the only legal access for mankind to enter into the Earth. The womb of the woman is the doorway, matrix, and stargate into the Earth and it is the Body of Christ's responsibility to inform every little girl how precious and important her ability to give life is. If the gift of giving life is exceptional, how much more is her right and privilege to mother the very life she gave birth to?

Eve

The mother of all living began in a certain location called the Garden of Eden. The only way we know where the Garden is located is by the names of the four rivers that extended from the Garden of Eden. Genesis 2:11 says, *"The name of the first (river) is Pison: that is it which compasseth the whole land of Havilah, where there is gold."* Havilah is present-day Zimbabwe, and it has the second largest gold reserve per square kilometer in the whole world. The second river is Gihon that compasses the whole land of Ethiopia. The third river is named Hiddekel, and it flows toward the east of Assyria (present-day Iraq, Syria, and Kuwait) and the fourth river is

Euphrates (which flows through Turkey to Syria). All of these rivers can be found in Genesis 2:11-14. Based on the evidence given by the four names of the rivers that flowed from the Garden of Eden, we can easily ascertain that the Garden of Eden was located in the territory of Africa which included what is known today as the Middle East (before Europeans named it the Middle East).

Anthropology is the study of the origins of human societies and cultures and has long determined that civilization began in Africa. I recently submitted my DNA to a reputable ancestry company and their worldwide database of human genetics is impressive. One of the pieces of genetic information that was submitted to me included this quote:

"Mitochondrial Eve, or at least the last living population group to match her genetic makeup, lived in East Africa 150,000 to 170,000 years ago. This haplogroup is limited to Eastern Africa and is believed to be the root of all shared maternal lineage, suggesting an ultimate origin of all modern human beings tracing back to Africa." Concerning the specificity of my Haplogroup they submitted this:

"Haplogroup F was one of the first haplogroups of modern humans to develop outside of Africa. It appeared about 43,800 – 56,800 years ago, right after the Out-of-Africa migration."

Ancestry companies openly admit that civilization began in Africa and migrated from there. We knew this truth from the very beginning by looking at the four rivers that proceeded from the Garden of Eden. If life began in Africa, we also know that God's first man and woman were Black. Eve was a Black woman and was the mother of all living. Yahweh chose a Black woman to birth civilizations and He chose Black women to birth His Hebrew bloodlines. Black is beautiful, gifted, and strong. The enemy has done such a good job changing this truth, especially when we look at the condition of the Black family here in America. Nevertheless, the first shall be last and the last shall be first. The truth of biblical Black History has systematically been silenced and censored for hundreds of years. However, the truth has always been right before our eyes written in black and white on the pages of Scripture.

2

Answer Key

And ye shall know the truth, and the truth shall make you free.
John 8:32

Before beginning, I would like to lay the ground rule: the Word of God is truth and is the final authority. I don't need extra biblical sources to prove to anyone what is plainly written in Scripture. Genesis chapter ten will be used as the Answer Key. An Answer Key indicates the correct answer provided by the question. It is a key to the answers (to a test or exercise). The definition of *answer* is, *something spoken or written in reply to a question*.[3] Noah Webster's definition of *key* is *that which serves to explain anything difficult to be understood*.[4] The proof that African women mothered all Hebrew bloodlines is found in the Answer Key of Genesis chapter ten. It is universally understood when it comes to blackness in people, "If it is in the roots, it is in the fruit."

After the worldwide flood of Noah's day, the Earth was repopulated by Noah's three sons (and their wives): Shem, Ham, and Japheth. Since it is scientifically and biologically impossible for two white people to produce Black offspring, common sense says that Noah's three sons and their wives could not have been all Caucasian, as seen in about every movie depicting their story and every other biblical story. Some may ask, "What proof do you have that any of Noah's sons were Black besides what was aforementioned?" Let's look to the Answer Key in Genesis 10, verses 1 and 6:

Now these are the generations of the sons of Noah, Shem, Ham, and Japheth: and unto them were sons born after the flood.

And the sons of Ham; Cush, and Mizraim, and Phut, and Canaan.

Almighty God created color and as the Master Colorist, He designed how color works. He created genetics and designed the function of chromosomes and dominant and recessive genes. His Divine composition determined that the gene in the Black man is more dominant than the genes He created in men of other colors. This does not make Black men more intelligent, moral, spiritual, or ethically superior. However, when it comes to color, black is dominant and all other human colors, (brown, red, yellow, and white) biologically, can come from black.

Pastor Walter Arthur McCray, who wrote *The Black Presence in the Bible* stated, "The reader will soon discover that Black people mentioned in Scripture may be identified 1) through names and adjectives; 2) through their ancestors, and family trees; 3) through extra biblical information gained from other areas of study, including archeology, anthropology, culture, etc.; and 4) through the chronological correlation with the Black ethnic makeup of peoples in the biblical world." (pg. 20)[5]

Names and meaning of names are great teachers and identifiers. We can confidently determine that Noah's son, Ham, was definitely a Black man and that each one of his sons were also Black. *Ham* in Hebrew means *black, hot, and swarthy (dark-skinned)*.[6] You might say, "That's not enough proof Ham was a Black man." The names of Ham's four sons further solidify their color. Ham's firstborn son's name is Cush and *Cush* is translated *Ethiopia*.[7] Ham's second son name is *Mizraim* and it is translated, *Egypt*.[8] Ham's third son is *Phut* which is translated, *Libya*.[9] Ham's fourth son is Canaan and Canaan Land is the original name and territory of what we know today as The Holy Land or Israel.[10] Are you convinced Ham was Black? Each of his son's names are African countries. Yes, that includes Israel. Before the Earth was divided into continents, the Earth was one mass of land. The division of land occurred after Noah's Flood. We can look to the Answer Key for proof. Genesis 10:25 says:

And unto Eber were born two sons: the name of one was Peleg; for in his days was the earth divided; and his brother's name was Joktan.

Before the Europeans came along thousands of years later and named this area of the world "the Middle East," all of the area including Israel, Jordan, Iraq, Saudi Arabia, Ethiopia, Turkey, Egypt, etc., was known as the land of Cush or Ethiopia. The name *Cush* in Hebrew means *burnt, fire like,* and *dark-skinned*.[11] There is no doubt Ham was a Black man and his sons were undeniably Black, also. As you read the Old Testament, especially the record of the Patriarchs: Abraham, Isaac, and Jacob, all the way to the prophetic books, the majority of the chosen peoples' allies and enemies came directly from the line of Ham. Judges 3:5-6 states:

And the children of Israel dwelt among the Canaanites, Hittites, and Amorites, and Perizzites, and Hivites, and Jebusites:

And they took their daughters to be their wives, and gave their daughters to their sons, and served their gods.

Who are these Canaanites, Hittites, Amorites, Perizzites, Hivites, and Jebusites? Let's check the Answer Key. Genesis 10:15-18 records:

And Canaan begat Sidon his first born, and Heth,

And the Jebusite, and the Amorite, and the Girgasite,

And the Hivite, and the Arkite, and the Sinite,

And the Arvadite, and the Zemarite, and the Hamathite: and afterward were the families of the Canaanites spread abroad.

As you can see, all of these ancient tribes came directly from Ham's fourth son, Canaan which makes them all African. Judges 3:6 states that the children of Israel took their daughters to be their wives. This happened many, many times throughout Israel's history. We tend to date, fall in love with, and marry those in close proximity to us. If you are Black and your children go to all-white schools, the likelihood they will date white classmates is very high. God called Abraham out of Ur of the Chaldees (or Chaldeans). Ur is modern day Iraq. Elohim called Abraham, Isaac, and Jacob to sojourn in the land of Canaan. Each of the Patriarchs married a woman from their native land and people. However, each of Jacob's twelve sons who became the twelve Tribes of Israel, married a Canaanite or Egyptian. Although the Patriarchs married within their family

(Sarah, Rebekah, Leah, and Rachel), each of the twelve sons of Jacob (that became the twelve Tribes of Israel), married African women. Each of Abraham's other sons by Hagar (Abraham's Egyptian wife), and Keturah, (the wife that Abraham took after Sarah died), married African women. This means each of the twelve Tribes of Israel were mothered by an African woman. This is quite startling because today the majority of those who call themselves Jews are European. Every chapter chronicling the Patriarch's lives are among the descendants of Ham. Genesis 12:6,10 says:

And Abram passed through the land unto the place of Sichem, unto the plain of Moreh. And the Canaanite was then in the land.

And there was a famine in the land: and Abram went down into Egypt to sojourn there; for the famine was grievous in the land.

Genesis 13:7,10 records:

And there was a strife between the herdmen of Abram's cattle and the herdmen of Lot's cattle: and the Canaanite and Perizzite dwelled then in the land.

And Lot lifted up his eyes, and beheld all the plain of Jordan, that it was well watered every where, before the LORD destroyed Sodom and Gomorrah, even as the garden of the LORD, like the land of Egypt, as thou comest unto Zoar.

Canaan was the fourth son of Ham. Egypt was the second son of Ham. Their lands were located where Abraham, Isaac, and Jacob sojourned all of their years. The land of Canaan was the territory God promised to give the children of Israel as an inheritance. Genesis 17:8 says:

And I will give unto thee, and to thy seed after thee, the land wherein thou art a stranger, all the land of Canaan, for an everlasting possession; and I will be their God.

Even the land of Sodom and Gomorrah were Black lands. These cities were covered in the territory of the Canaanites. The Answer Key proves it.

And the border of the Canaanites was from Sidon, as thou comest to Gerar, unto Gaza; as thou goest unto Sodom, and Gomorrah, and Admah, and Zeboim, even unto Lasha. Genesis 10:19

Genesis 20:1 says, *"And Abraham journeyed from thence toward the south country, and dwelled between Kadesh and Shur, and sojourned in Gerar."* Gerar is listed as a territory of Canaan in the Answer Key. Genesis 21:34 says, *"And Abraham sojourned in the Philistines' land many days."* Who are the Philistines? The Answer Key explains. Genesis 10:13-14 says:

And Mizraim begat Ludim, and Anamim, and Lehabim, and Naphtuhim,

And Pathrusim, and Casluhim, (out of whom came Philistim,) and Caphtorim.

Remember, Mizraim is Ham's second son and the same as Egypt. It is Egypt's descendants who produced the Philistines, Israel's greatest enemy. Egypt is, of course, a part of Africa and they enslaved the children of Israel for hundreds of years. All races of people were on the Earth. However, the Bible chronicles the life and movement of God's chosen people, Israel. The Israelites occupied a limited geographical area that happens to be predominantly African, and the Israelites were promised a land that "flowed with milk and honey." This land belonged to Ham's fourth son, Canaan. The original name for the land of Israel was Canaan Land and it was 100% Black.

Nimrod

The most famous ancient kingdoms that existed after the Flood were established by a Black man. His name was Nimrod, and he was the first king and world ruler after the great Flood. He built the kingdoms of Assyria, Babylon, and even Nineveh. These kingdoms became very powerful and later on were attributed to the bloodline of Noah's son Shem, but it was a Black king who built and established them. The Answer Key proves this:

And Cush begat Nimrod: he began to be a mighty one in the earth.

He was a mighty hunter before the LORD: wherefore it is said, Even as Nimrod the mighty hunter before the LORD.

And the beginning of his kingdom was Babel, and Erech, and Accad, and Calneh, in the land of Shinar.

Out of that land went forth Asshur, and builded Ninevah, and the city of Rehoboth, and Calah.
Genesis 10:8-11

Abraham's father's name was Terah, and he was Nimrod's second in command. *Chaldeans* is another name for *Babylonians*.[12] This was the land Abraham was divinely called out of to follow Elohim. Civilization began in Africa and after Noah's Flood, civilization continued in the same areas. Civilization in Africa was built and led by Black people. There is no doubt the Old Testament is the history of Black people in Black lands. The name *Canaan* is mentioned eighty-nine times in the Bible. While *Canaanites* is mentioned sixty-seven times. The entire territory of all of Canaan's descendants is referred repeatedly in Scripture as *Canaan* or *the land of Canaan*. Yahweh allowed Noah's sons and grandsons to be identified and named by their territories. In the same way, all the territory of present-day Africa and the Middle East were originally called *Cush* (*Ethiopia*), because Nimrod was the first builder and king of the kingdoms of these areas.

Why God Chose Abram

For I know him, that he will command his children and his household after him, and they shall keep the way of the LORD, to do justice and judgment; that the LORD may bring upon Abraham that which he hath spoken of him.
Genesis 18:19

Yahweh chose Abram for the reasons mentioned in this passage: he would command his children and his household after Yahweh. He knew Abram would be faithful to teach everyone under his authority the ways of Elohim. Abram did not limit the training of his children to Isaac and Jacob, Abram trained his entire household, including all of his seed and his servants. This means he taught the ways of Yahweh not only to Sarah and Isaac, but also to his other wives, Hagar and Keturah and their sons. The knowledge of the One True God was known and spread because of Abram, the Father of Faith. This is how many important characters in Old Testament Scripture knew Yahweh for themselves; they were descendants of Abram, and he was faithful to teach them to worship the God of Heaven and Earth.

3

Hagar

Flight; Fugitive; Wanderer

And Sarai Abram's wife took Hagar her maid the Egyptian, after Abram had dwelt ten years in the land of Canaan and gave her to her husband Abram to be his wife.
Genesis 16:3

Who are Hebrews?

Before I delve into the firstborn of Abram, I need to first explain who the Hebrews are considered to be based on Scripture. The first time the word *Hebrew* is mentioned in the Bible, it is referring to Abram as "the Hebrew." This is recorded in Genesis 14:13:

And there came one that had escaped, and told Abram the Hebrew; for he dwelt in the plain of Mamre the Amorite, brother of Eshcol, and brother of Aner: and these were confederate with Abram.

Yahweh sovereignly chose to call Abram the first Hebrew. Therefore, there is no doubt the Father of the Faith was a Hebrew. The bloodline comes from the man. This is why the wife, and the children take the last name of the father in the family because the man is the one who possesses the seed and the bloodline. Now that we know Abram is the Hebrew, we know that he possesses the bloodline of all future Hebrews. In other words, all of Abram's children are Hebrews. This means Isaac, Jacob, and the twelve Tribes of Israel aren't the only Hebrews, but Abram's firstborn son, Ishmael and his descendants are Hebrews. In addition, Abram's six sons by his third wife Keturah, are Hebrews also. There are close to a billion Hebrews on Earth today. *Abram* means *great father* and God changed his name to *Abraham* meaning *father of many nations*.[13] How did he become a Father of many nations? Abraham had eight sons by three different wives and all of them are considered Hebrews.

Hebrew, Israelite, & Jew

Today, most people simply group Jews, Hebrews, and Israelites all together. However, there are distinctive differences between the three. In order to be a Hebrew, you must be from the bloodline of Abraham. In order to be an Israelite, you must be of the bloodline of the twelve Tribes of Israel. A Jew is technically those who come from the bloodline of the Tribe of Judah. This means if you are from the Tribe of Judah, you are a Jew, an Israelite, and a Hebrew. If you are from one of the other eleven Tribes of Israel, you are an Israelite and a Hebrew. And if you are from the descendants of one of Abraham's sons other than the twelve Tribes of Israel, you are a Hebrew but not an Israelite or a Jew. Don't judge someone who says they are Hebrew because the odds are quite possible, they are. Our ignorance concerning this is greater than the likelihood they are not. We have been ignorantly led to believe that the descendants of the twelve Tribes of Israel are the only Hebrews. However, the truth of the matter is, there are many, many Hebrews.

Hagar, the Egyptian

The Scripture is clear that Abram's second wife was an Egyptian. Egyptians are, of course, African despite many European powers attempting to separate Egypt from any reference to Africa itself. Looking to the Answer Key, Egypt (Mizraim) was the second son of Noah's son, *Ham*, whose name means *black, hot, swarthy* and *dark-skinned*.[14] The first son of Abram, was by his African Egyptian wife, Hagar. *Hagar* means *foreigner* or *stranger*.[15] Abram acquired Hagar as one of the many gifts from Pharoah, King of Egypt when he sojourned to Egypt during the great famine. (Genesis 12:16). God promised to bless Abram with the promised seed of Isaac through his first wife, Sarai. However, Abram's and Sarai's faith faltered as they waited for the promise. Sarai decided to help God out and requested that Abram take her fine, voluptuous Egyptian handmaiden as his wife in order to raise up seed. Of course, this was not what Yahweh instructed them. He very specifically told both of them that He would use Sarai to have the promised seed. Imagine being Abram and your already beautiful wife comes to you and requests that you marry her absolutely gorgeous handmaiden in order to have a son. As righteous as the Father of Faith was, he was still a man and jumped at the opportunity to marry this fine Egyptian woman and procreate with her.

Genesis 16:15 says:

And Hagar bare Abram a son: and Abram called his son's name, which Hagar bare, Ishmael.

Ishmael became the father of the Arab people. His father Abram was a Hebrew. Therefore, Ishmael and all of his descendants were Hebrew. Ishmael's mother was Egyptian which means Arab people are Hebrew and African. Hagar was the first mother of the Hebrew people. *Black Wives Matter* because Elohim sovereignly chose them to mother the Hebrew people of the Earth. It is not a coincidence that besides Sarai, each of the women who propagated the Hebrew bloodline would be African women. Hagar was just the first of many. This truth is important, especially for this generation of Black women who are neglected, ostracized and discounted throughout the world. Shades of Blackness are still judged according to lightness of skin color. There is an old saying, *"White is right. Light is alright. But Black must get back."* I'm reminded of the Grammy Awards of 2002 when the darker skinned songwriter, singer, and musician, India Arie was nominated for seven Grammys and did not win a single one. However, the lighter skinned songwriter, singer, and musician, Alicia Keys, won five Grammys.[16] Both were amazing and gifted new artists, but the snub of India Arie was hurtful and brazenly transparent clearly showing us who the White Europeans preferred.

Yahweh not only saw the gifts and strengths of His Cushite women, but He also understood the purpose of their Blackness pertaining to genetics. In a world today where Blackness has systematically been demonized by Europeans who possess recessive genetics, Yehovah has time stamped His approval of African women in His Holy Word by choosing them to birth Hebrew tribes. Ishmael could have been birthed by any number of women, but Elohim predestined that the progenitor of the Arab race would be mothered by an African woman named Hagar. A Black woman named Eve gave birth to the first humans and Black women continued to birth civilizations, proving that *Black Wives Matter.*

Immediately after Hagar knew she was pregnant with the Patriarch's firstborn, she despised Sarai. Most likely, Hagar no longer felt like a common servant and handmaiden. Now she had the upper hand. In her mind, Sarai was now subservient to her and maybe she thought Abram's affection would shift from Sarai to her. This proved to be a terrible miscalculation by Hagar. Sarai received permission from Abram to handle Hagar as she pleased, and Sarai roughed her up and kicked her out of the house. Although Abram desired his firstborn by Hagar to be the promised seed, Sarai, and his lack of trust in what God promised them did not change God's mind. Genesis 17:18 says:

And Abraham said unto God, O that Ishmael might live before thee!

Life in the Womb

After Sarai dealt harshly with Hagar, Hagar fled into the wilderness. God visited Hagar by a fountain of water in the wilderness. Elohim did not have to intervene and speak to Hagar, but He wanted us to know that *Black Wives Matter*, so He scheduled a special counseling session just for this confused, young African queen. Yahweh did not excuse her disrespect of Sarai but comforted her and spoke to the great destiny she carried in her womb. I would like to interject a word about the preciousness of life in the womb. When a woman conceives, she not only carries life in her womb, but she is pregnant with future generations and a nation. When

Rebekah was pregnant with Esau and Jacob, Yahweh spoke these words to her:

And the LORD said unto her, Two nations are in thy womb, and two manner of people shall be separated from thy bowels; and the one people shall be 3stronger than the other people; and the elder shall serve the younger. Genesis 25:23

Yahweh took the time out to explain to Hagar the character and nature of her son, Ishmael, after He told her that she needed to return and submit to Sarai. He also spoke to Ishmael's greatness. Genesis 16:10 says:

And the angel of the LORD said unto her, I will multiply thy seed exceedingly, that it shall not be numbered for multitude.

Yahweh not only corrected her, but He affirmed her and prophesied concerning her son's great destiny. This is the conversation between Yahweh and Hagar about the destiny of all Arab people. Yahweh met her in her hour of distress and made sure she aligned herself properly in Abraham's house. This is important because He could have allowed Hagar to be discarded and never mentioned again, but He did not. Elohim destined that Abraham would be the Father of Many Nations and the precious life in Hagar's womb was the first fulfillment of that prophecy. Before *Black Lives* can *Matter*, *Black Wives* must *Matter*. We have to recognize who the real enemy is and who promotes, finances, and legalizes the murder of life in the womb. Whether or not children are planned, they are precious and deserve to live. From the beginning of time, God has taken people who were born in the worst situations and empowered them to overcome their circumstances and live full and victorious lives. Hagar could have given up. However, she did not because Elohim visited her to remind us that *Black Wives Matter*. Hagar is now spoken of by every generation as the mother of all Hebrew, Arab people.

Laughter for Laughter

When Abram was seventy-five years old, Elohim promised Abram a son from Sarai. Elohim visited Sarai and opened her womb to receive the promised seed of Isaac when Abram was ninety-nine years old. Nine months later, Sarai gave birth to her miracle son Isaac, and at his birth, Abram is one hundred years old. In essence, Abram had to wait twenty-five years before God's promise to him came to fruition. Once the promised seed of Isaac arrived in Abram and Sarai's home, and when Isaac turned five, the age when he was weaned off his mother's milk, Abram threw a celebration for Isaac and there was a clear paradigm shift. Genesis 21:9-14 informs us:

And Sarah saw the son of Hagar the Egyptian, which she had born unto Abraham, mocking.

Wherefore she said unto Abraham, Cast out this bondwoman and her son: for the son of this bondwoman shall not be heir with my son, even with Isaac.

And the thing was very grievous in Abraham's sight because of his son.

And God said unto Abraham, Let it not be grievous in thy sight because of the lad, and because of thy bondwoman; in all that Sarah hath said unto thee, hearken unto her voice; for in Isaac shall thy seed be called.

And also of the son of the bondwoman will I make a nation, because he is thy seed.

And Abraham rose up early in the morning, and took bread, and a bottle of water, and gave it unto Hagar, putting it on her shoulder, and the child, and sent her away: and she departed, and wandered in the wilderness of Beersheba.

Ishmael was thirteen years old when God changed Abram's name to Abraham (Genesis 17:5,25) and initiated the covenant symbol of circumcision for Abraham and his entire household of men. (Genesis 17:7-14) The next year, Isaac was born which would make Ishmael fourteen at Isaac's birth. Five years later is when Abraham threw the celebration for Isaac which would make Ishmael nineteen years old. So, at the age of nineteen, Ishmael mocked Isaac. Think about this. A nineteen-year-old is making fun of his five-year-old brother. This behavior is what sparked Sarah to go to Abraham and request that Hagar and her son be removed from their responsibility. What is interesting is the meaning of the word *mocking*. It is the same root word as from the word *laughing* when Abram and Sarai began *laughing* upon hearing Elohim promise that Sarai would give birth to a son in her old age. This is how and why God chose to name the child, Isaac. *Isaac* means *laughter*.[17] Therefore, Hagar and Ishmael were banished permanently because Ishmael *laughed* at the one named *laughter*. How ironic.

Having married and bore Abraham's firstborn son, Hagar had to feel some degree of security and lifelong protection. Abraham was one of the richest men of his time. What happened to Hagar had to be devastating. Only this time, there would be no returning back to the fold. Most likely, no one in Abraham's caravan ever thought that Sarah would give birth to a son. Once she did, the clock began ticking for Hagar and Ishmael. Abraham's heart broke when he had to kick out his firstborn son and his second wife, Hagar. God spoke to Abraham and instructed him to do as Sarah demanded and Abraham released them definitively. Another interesting detail is how one of the wealthiest men of that day sent his second wife and firstborn son away with nothing but bread and water. One more interesting morsel is how Scripture repeatedly called the nineteen-year-old Ishmael *a child* (*a lad*), after they were banished from Abraham's home. Scripture never acknowledges Ishmael as a mature male who has reached adulthood. The account reads like Ishmael is Isaac's age.

Ishmael's Egyptian Wife

And he dwelt in the wilderness of Paran: and his mother took him a wife out of the land of Egypt.
Genesis 21:21

The firstborn son of Abraham, the Hebrew, and the first to continue the Hebrew bloodline is Ishmael. And Ishmael married another African woman. He is the progenitor of the Arab race. Ishmael's mother was an African and the mother of his children was African, also. Ishmael, the progenitor of all Arab people was half Semitic and half African. Since Ishmael is half African, and his wife was African, his descendants are three-fourths African and one-fourth Semitic. God visited Hagar a second time once she and Ishmael were permanently evicted from Abraham's home. Elohim did not have to visit her either time she was removed. However, He did. And the reason was, first, He loved her, and second, she had a major part to play in Abraham becoming the Father of many nations. The first nation Abraham became the father of was the Arab nation. This means all Arabian people are Hebrews. Did you know the Quran does not include any lineages of leaders or people groups? The Bible gives us Ishmael's lineage.

Now these are the generations of Ishmael. Abraham's son, whom Hagar the Egyptian, Sarah's handmaid, bare unto Abraham:

And these are the names of the sons of Ishmael, by their names, according to their generations: the firstborn of Ishmael, Nebajoth; and Kedar, and Adbeel, and Mibsam.

And Mishma, and Dumah, and Massa,

Hadar, and Tema, Jetur, Naphish, and Kedemah:

These are the sons of Ishmael, and these are their names, by their towns, and by their castles; twelve princes according to their nations.

And these are the years of the life of Ishmael, an hundred and thirty and seven years: and he gave up the ghost and died; and was gathered unto his people.
Genesis 25:12-17

Only the Word of God gives us the detailed lineage of our forefathers. These lists of names are so meticulous and accurate and go back thousands of years. Only Yahweh could do this. As I cover the bloodline of each of the Hebrew groups fathered by Abraham, you will discover that many of them had something in common: they had twelve sons. Twelve is the number of governments. Ishmael had twelve princes. Esau had twelve dukes. Jacob had twelve sons, and this established their tribal identities and governments in the earth. This book is going to prove that each Hebrew male married an African wife. This means Africa is deeply rooted in all of the Hebrew people.

4

Keturah

Incense; Fragrant Smoke; Fragrance; Perfume; and Aloe wood

Then again Abraham took a wife, and her name was Keturah. Genesis 25:1

The Scriptures say Hagar and Keturah married Abraham and were his wives. However, each of them maintained the status of concubine or handmaiden. It is clear they did not have the same status as Sarah because they would not bare the promised seed. Some scholars have tried to make Hagar and Keturah the same person. They presume Hagar returned to Abraham after Sarah died under a different name. This is not true. Keturah was a different woman from a different area. However, she was still African. Keturah was a Black woman, and she was from Ethiopia. We know she was Black because she gave Abraham Midian, one of their six sons. Midian is the Father of the Midianites, Black people who had history with the children of Israel. The Kenites were a tribe within the Midianite family, and they were engrafted into the Tribe of Judah. We will go into greater detail about this later.

Keturah

The name *Keturah* means *incense, fragrant smoke, perfume,* and *aloe-wood.*[18] Abraham had just lost the love of his life of 40 years and the mother of the promised seed of Isaac. The life of the Father of Faith was full of ups and downs, life and death, and happiness and drama. Abraham was a very rich man, but he made many mistakes. Many believe the constant tensions in the Middle East are directly connected to Abraham's loss of faith when he married Hagar and produced Ishmael. The descendants of Ishmael and Isaac are still fighting today. Ishmael is still mocking Isaac 3,500 years later. The prophecy from Yahweh in Genesis 16:12 concerning Ishmael is still resounding throughout the ages:

And he will be a wild man; his hand will be against every man, and every man's hand against him; and he shall dwell in the presence of all his brethren.

God Hears

The war between Israel and surrounding Arab nations and the constant fighting between tribes within the Arab world is proof that the prophetic utterance concerning Ishmael is true. *Ishmael* means *whom God hears*.[19] God heard Ishmael's mother's cry when she was sent away from Abraham's home the first time and He heard Hagar's cry the second time, too. Yahweh not only heard Hagar's cries of pain, needs, and desperation but He hears the cry of all Black mothers who have been forgotten and counted out. He hears the Black mothers who are abandoned by the fathers of their children, rejected by their family, and expected to fail in life. Yahweh has always heard their cry and will continue to hear them. He not only hears their cry but moves in compassion to visit them and reminds them that every life is precious, and He has a plan and purpose for her and her children.

After mourning for Sarah, Abraham was due for a new season, and a fresh start. The stink of death not only lingered in the atmosphere from the season of mourning Sarah's death but within the soul of the Patriarch. Death has a way of procrastinating as it works through our mind and emotions. Death is a part of life, but it desires to live and procreate in our hearts because of its pain. However, Abraham did something prophetic we all need to do after taking time to go through the grieving process. After his great loss, Abraham buried the dead out of his sight.

I am a stranger and a sojourner with you: give me a possession of a buryingplace with you, that I may bury my dead out of my sight. Genesis 23:4

Fortunately, mental health awareness has been highlighted in our society as of late. The poor and oppressed suffer the most in life and need mental health therapy. A great part of mental health is not just suffering the blows of life but learning how to go through all the stages of the grieving process and in the end, how to bury the dead out of our sight. Promotion always proceeds great tests. Abraham had many tests in his life, but the death of his beloved wife Sarah proved to be one of the most profound. Yahweh did not leave the Father of the Faith comfortless. Yahweh blessed and promoted Abraham, and it came in the form of another beautiful African wife named Keturah.

Perfumery

The word *perfume* comes from the prefix, *per* meaning, *through* in Latin and *fume* or *fumus* means smoke in Latin.[20] The first form of perfume was incense. Perfumery is the art or process of making perfume.[21] As we look into this ancient process, we will discover its prophetic nature in the life of Abraham that qualified him for Keturah (perfume, incense, and fragrant smoke). The first perfume maker on record was an Egyptian chemist, a woman named Tapputi. Stories of her have been found on a clay tablet from Mesopotamia suggesting that perfume was invented by her sometime during the second millennium BC.[22] Early perfume was made using natural materials such as leaves, seeds, flowers, wood, bark, frankincense, myrrh, and roots. Civilizations have used perfumes and fragrances in different ways. Some cultures used perfume to distinguish nobility and only the upper classes had access to perfumed products because it was expensive to create them. Perfumes were used for hygiene and cleanliness, as well as ceremonial purposes. Egyptians associated their perfumes with their gods.

The aroma therapy of Keturah in Abraham's life not only produced another son in his old age, but six sons. We hear about the phenomenal faith it took for Abraham to have the promised seed of Isaac at one hundred years old, but we rarely hear about the faith it took for Abraham to have six additional sons at one hundred and thirty years old. This story is just as important and speaks to the impressive role his Black wife Keturah played in his life and in the life of all men who were blessed to know her. In contrast to what envious and racist European people have successfully propagandized the world to believe about Yahweh's Black women, from the very beginning of mankind, these Cushite women have been the perfume, incense, fragrant smoke, and aloe wood to all of humanity. The attacks against her and her unborn children are so intense because the enemy has witnessed time and time again the power and purpose that has proceeded from her womb. What if Mary had an abortion? The hatred that was prophesied concerning the woman's seed and the serpent's seed is alive and more palpable now than ever.

Keturah is prophetic of Yeshua because He is our Fragrance and Incense. We came to Him reeking of sin and death having been "born in sin and shapen in iniquity." The Scriptures inform us that "...all our righteousnesses are as filthy rags." We were all spiritually dead, cursed with the stench of the promise of hell, but because of the work of Calvary, Yeshua took our dirty rags and the stink of our sin in exchange for His glorious perfume of the Only Begotten of Yahweh. Can you imagine how Almighty God smells? When we repent and ask Yeshua into our hearts, we are not only taking on His righteousness, but also His Fragrance. If you are a follower of Yeshua, you smell like God. God presented Keturah to Abraham signifying that every area of his life had a brand new, remarkable aroma and only the residents of Heaven would recognize this Fragrance that signifies resurrection.

Keturah's sons

And she bare him Zimran, and Jokshan, and Medan, and Midian, and Ishbak, and Shuah. Genesis 25:2

There is a great lesson to be seen in Abraham having six more sons with Keturah many years after having Isaac and that is, if you do something once, you can do it again and again. This is the power of knowledge. If you learn how to buy a home, it doesn't matter how many financial setbacks you experience, it is just a matter a time before you will be able to do it again because you already learned the process and have been through the steps. Abraham understood how faith works and the importance of patience. Therefore, after Sarah died, he was still walking by faith and more than likely, his faith increased. His reward was six more sons because the Word of the Lord that he would become the Father of many nations was not yet fulfilled.

Six is the number of man because man was created on the sixth day. Keturah's six sons solidified her husband's prophecy of being the Father of many nations. Six sons meant another six nations. Elohim choreographed that all tribes connected to Abraham's Hebrew bloodline would be mothered by His African woman, Keturah. Abraham was definitely a man of color and his six sons by this wonderful Black woman not only produced six extra Hebrew bloodlines, but six more Black tribes who would become a part of the Arabian and African nations.

Keturah was a concubine which means she was with Abraham for some time and saw with her own eyes many of the experiences he had with Elohim. She could have been there when God personally visited him. Abe was an exception to the rule: he was rich and believed in God. He was educated but was not an educated fool. Keturah knew how special the Father of Faith was and had no problem accepting the honor of fulfilling the last part of making him the Father of many nations. Keturah mothered six sons who would be taught about the One True God and spread it throughout the Earth. Everything in life starts with a seed and Yahweh is never in a rush. Keturah, who represented the sweet-smelling perfume and incense in this season of Abraham's life, culminated his legacy with six amazing sons to continue the Hebrew bloodline who would perpetuate the nature and culture of the God of Heaven and Earth. Hagar only gave Abraham one son. Sarah only gave him one son. Keturah revealed The Most High's awesome grace by giving the world six new sons to continue the Hebrew bloodline.

Midian

Midian, the fourth son of Abraham and Keturah, is spoken of frequently in Scripture. However, there isn't much mentioned concerning the other sons, but history shows they blended among their cousins: Ishmael and his twelve princes of the Arabian people. Yahweh desired to have the promised seed of Isaac and his descendants separate from the rest of Abraham's seed. Genesis 25:6 says:

But unto the sons of the concubines, which Abraham had, Abraham gave gifts, and sent them away from Isaac his son, while he yet lived, eastward, unto the east country.

Elohim promised the descendants of Isaac, the land of Canaan. The territory we know today as Israel was originally inhabited by Africans called the Canaanites. What is called the Middle East was originally part of the land of Cush. Cush was Ham's firstborn son. What we call Africa, once included all the land of Israel to Iraq. God's decisions are not based on what happens in time, but His will is decided beforehand or what Scripture calls foreknowledge or predestination. In other words, although Noah cursed Canaan to serve Shem and Japheth, Canaan's descendants did not lose their land to the children of Israel (because of what Canaan did to Noah), because Yahweh had already decided it before the foundation of the world. From the time Noah declared Divine judgment against Canaan's lineage, it would actually be 1,500 years before it was fulfilled. Abraham, Isaac, and Jacob sojourned in Canaan Land instead of possessing it for two reasons. Number one, they were not numerous enough to actually conquer and fill the land. Number two, God's predetermined season for the Canaanites to occupy the land was not yet complete. God spoke concerning this while cutting covenant with Abraham in Genesis 15:16:

But in the fourth generation they shall come hither again: for the iniquity of the Amorites is not yet full.

Keturah was African and Abraham was Semitic and Hebrew. Therefore, their offspring would be African Hebrews. Scripture proves this when their son Midian, who became the Father of the Midianites, is mentioned. They are referred to in unison with the Cushites. Habakkuk 3:7 says, *"I saw the tents of Cushan in affliction: and the curtains of the land of Midian did tremble."* Tents were made of animal skins in biblical days. The larger tents had multiple rooms that were divided from each other by goat hair curtains. This reference by the Prophet Habakkuk of tents and curtains, which were made from the same substance, is revealing how the Cushites and the Midianites are in the same family. Numbers 12:1 says:

And Miriam and Aaron spake against Moses because of the Ethiopian woman whom he had married: for he had married an Ethiopian woman.

Remember Cush is translated Ethiopian; they are the same. But the Scriptures say that Moses married a Midianite (Exodus 2:16-21). Again, we have Cushite (Ethiopian) and Midianite referring to the same woman who Moses married. The Midianites were Black people because Abraham was a man of color and Keturah his wife was African. Since this is the truth concerning Midian, it must be true concerning the other five sons, also. The same is true concerning Noah and his three sons. If Noah and his wife (Joan of Ark) produced a very dark-skinned son named Ham, Shem and Japheth had to be, at least men of color, and at best Black men because it is absolutely impossible for two Caucasian people to have Black offspring. God wanted there to be no doubt that His chosen people Israel and all other Hebrew bloodlines were Black.

Sheba and Dedan

Abraham's and Keturah's second born son's name was Jokshan. Genesis 25:3 says, *"And Jokshan begat Sheba, and Dedan..."* These two names are also mentioned in the line of Ham under the sons of Cush. Genesis 10:7 says, *"And the sons of Cush; Seba, Havilah, and Sabtah, and Raamah, and Sabtechah: and the sons of Raamah; Sheba, and Dedan."* These two names are mentioned together in both Cush's and Jokshan's (son of Abraham and Keturah) lineage. This is not a coincidence; it is another documented witness of the relation between these two African tribes. Evidently, Keturah knew her ancestry and told it to her sons and they were in proximity to them and lived among some of their relatives. Sheba is used many times in connection to Black people and Black nations. David married a Black woman named Bathsheba and their union produced Solomon (a Black man). Solomon later married the Queen of Sheba who was from the land of Ethiopia. Sheba and Dedan came from the bloodline of Abraham, and therefore were Hebrew. Although they were African and Hebrew, they became a part of the growing Arabian Tribes when Abraham separated his son Ishmael (from Hagar) and his six sons (from Keturah) away from Isaac and sent them to the east. Isaiah 21:13 says, *"The burden upon Arabia. In the forest of Arabia shall ye lodge, O ye travelling companies of Dedanim."*

5

Esau's Wives

Judith, Praise Yehovah

Bashemath, Fragrance

Aholibama, Tent of the High Place

Mahalath, Stringed Instrument

Esau's Wives

Isaac had twin sons: Esau and Jacob. This means the descendants of Esau would also be Hebrew. And yes, Esau married African wives also. Isaac admonished Jacob not to marry Canaanite women (Genesis 28:1). However, these fine, Black African queens were too irresistible. Esau had already married two Canaanite wives. The land of Canaan was an ancient Atlanta, Georgia. Seeing is believing! Esau married two Hittite wives. The Answer Key of Genesis chapter ten will inform us who the Hittites were:

And Canaan begat Sidon his first born, and Heth.
Genesis 10:15

Heth is the Father of the Hittites, and because he is one of Canaan's sons, they are also an African, Canaanite Tribe. Genesis 26:34-35 says:

And Esau was forty years old when he took to wife Judith the daughter of Beeri the Hittite, and Bashemath the daughter of Elon the Hittite:

Which were a grief of mind to Isaac and to Rebekah.

Esau's first two wives were African women. Their names were Judith and Bashemath. The name *Judith* is the feminine of Judah and *Judah* means *praise*.[23] *Bashemath* means *spice and fragrance*.[24] How was it that two beautiful Black women called *Praise* and *Spice* and *Fragrance* could be "a grief of mind" to

Esau's mother and father? I do not know. Maybe they were too voluptuous, outspoken, and sassy like many Black women are today. Or they served the false gods many of the Canaanites worshipped. Could it be they were some of the Instagram models of their day? Bashemath's modeling name could have been *Spice*. Bashemath is also called by the name Adah in Genesis 36:2. *Adah* means *beauty, comeliness, adornment, ornament,* and *pleasure*.[25] Genesis 36:2 reads:

Esau took his wives of the daughters of Canaan; Adah the daughter of Elon the Hittite, and Aholibamah the daughter of Anah the daughter of Zibeon the Hivite.

Esau's wife, Aholibamah, whose name means *tent of the high place* was a Hivite and the Answer Key of Genesis 10:17 informs us that Hivites are another African, Canaanite Tribe.[26] "And the Hivite, the Arkite, and the Sinite." Genesis 28:8-9 records another African wife of Esau:

And Esau seeing that the daughters of Canaan pleased not Isaac his father;

Then went Esau unto Ishmael, and took unto the wives which he had Mahalath the daughter of Ishmael Abraham's son, the sister of Nebajoth, to be his wife.

Esau also married another Egyptian African named Mahalath whose name means *beautifully adorned; mild, smooth; pleasing to the touch; rhythmic movements; sweet,* and *harmonious sounds*.[27] Regardless that Abraham and Isaac did not desire for their sons to marry Canaanite women (because they did not want their sons to practice idolatry), it seems these gorgeous Black women were simply enchanting, intelligent, alluring, and ravishing. If we draw characteristics from their names, we can conclude Esau's African wives were beautiful, pleasing to the touch, spicy, fragrant, comely, a tent of high places, rhythmic, sweet, harmonious, and praisers.

Edomites

Esau became known as Edom and his descendants were called Edomites. Genesis 36:1 says, *"Now these are the generations of Esau, who is Edom."* He received the name Edom (meaning red) not because he came out his mother's womb as a red baby, but because he sold his birthright to his younger brother Jacob for a bowl of red pottage. Genesis 25:30 records:

And Esau said to Jacob, Feed me, I pray thee, with that same red pottage; for I am faint: therefore was his name called Edom.

Tensions ran high after Esau sold his birthright to Jacob. Jacob finally solidified it by tricking his father Isaac to speak the firstborn blessing over him. Esau forfeited his birthright to Jacob, but it meant nothing unless Jacob could get his father to declare the firstborn blessing over him. After Jacob and his mother Rebekah colluded to apprehend this blessing from Isaac, Esau found out about it and for many years hated Jacob and desired to kill him. Jacob fled for his life and years later after Jacob married Leah and Rachel and had his sons, he reunited with his elder brother Esau, and they made peace. (Genesis 33) Esau had twelve sons by his four African wives and established the nation of Edom. Genesis 36:15-19 records the Dukes of Edom that created their nation:

These were the dukes of the sons of Esau: the sons of Eliphaz the firstborn son of Esau; duke Teman, duke Omar, duke Zepho, duke Kenaz,

Duke Korah, duke Gatam, and duke Amalek; these are the dukes that came of Eliphaz in the land of Edom; these were the sons of Adah.

And these are the sons of Reuel Esau's son; duke Nahath, duke Zerah, duke Shammah, duke Mizzah: these are the dukes that came to Reuel in the land of Edom; these are the sons of Bashemath Esau's wife.

And these are the sons of Aholibamah Esau's wife; duke Jeush, duke Jaalam, duke Korah: these were the dukes that came of Aholibamah the daughter of Anah, Esau's wife.

These are the sons of Esau, who is Edom, and these are their dukes.

Through Esau, God had established another Hebrew line of descent and it was exclusively mothered by African women: three Canaanite wives and one Egyptian wife, all from the line of Ham. There is no doubt, the purpose of Yahweh is clearly seen in that every single family of Hebrew ancestry originated from African wives and mothers. The lengths the European clergy of the church have taken to either hide this irrefutable truth or make revisionist documentation is purely evil. How could a people (the Europeans) who do not even appear in biblical history until the New Testament have duped the world concerning the presence and purpose of Elohim's Black people in Scripture? This is definitely worth shouting from the mountaintop. The Europeans' racism and inferiority complex goes so deep that they were willing to create a theory called evolution whereby they believed mankind were descendants of apes, instead of accepting the truth of God's Word that clearly shows all civilization proceeded from Black people and a Black land.

Think of the most famous pastors and teachers of today, and out of the hundreds or thousands of great messages they have taught, can you name one teaching they have done telling the truth about the overwhelming evidence of Blackness in the Bible, especially in the Old Testament? Many of these famous leaders have doctorate degrees in Theology and Divinity. Therefore, they are not ignorant concerning this truth. That means, these pastors and teachers intentionally decided not to teach it. The *Cancel Culture* conveniently looked past evangelicals' blatant revisions of the whole Bible. Ninety-nine percent of all biblical movies and series depict the main characters and tribes as Caucasians instead of Blacks. The Christian anime television series, *Superbook* was produced by *Tatsunoko Productions*, and *TV Tokyo* in Japan in conjunction with Christian Broadcast Network (CBN) in America. This biblical anime production depicts all the characters in

European shades while only satan and his angels have dark skin. Based on Genesis chapter ten's list of nations, white and yellow people are the descendants of Noah's son Japheth who produced the Caucasian and Asian race. Isn't it interesting that Caucasian and Asian companies came together to produce a biblical anime series about African and Black people in Scripture but miraculously made everyone look like them instead of what the Bible clearly says they are - Black? And everyone seems shocked when glancing upon an image of the Last Supper with all Black men. The European Church hierarchy has brainwashed and whitewashed the masses. Black people actually display pictures of White Jesus on their walls.

LEMBA JEWISH TRIBE

The Gateway Center for Israel posted a video on February 6, 2018, titled, *The Lemba Jewish Tribe: Prophecy Fulfilled*.

"The Lemba Tribe lives in Zimbabwe and South Africa and are direct descendants of the twelve Tribes of Israel. The Assyrians conquered the Northern Kingdom of Israel in 1 Kings and dispersed them throughout Assyrian territories. The Assyrians murdered many of the Israelites. Some of the people of Yahweh assimilated into the Assyrian culture, while others fled. This is connected to the origins of the lost Tribes of Israel. The Lemba Tribe secured their rich Jewish culture through oral tradition. They believe their tribe is the bloodline of Levi and the Levitical Priesthood. They teach how they fled and migrated to Yemen where they became traders and craftsmen until they were forced to escape war again. Then, they crossed the Red Sea to Africa. As they journeyed down through Africa, they built great cities of stone. Archeologists have verified the existence of these cities through the many artifacts that have been discovered (which contain) Jewish designs.

The Lemba Tribe is like no other African Tribe because of their strict adherence to Jewish customs. Despite losing their original Torah during their journey from Israel to Zimbabwe, all oral traditions have been maintained, such as, dietary laws (including kosher standards and restrictions on certain meats), circumcision on the eighth day, and traditional rabbinical clothing. These African Jews who call themselves original Jews are committed to the ways of Yahweh that have been passed down from generation to generation.

Eventually, DNA testing was able to validate the Lemba Tribe's claims. Dr. Tudor Parfitt of the University of London, swabbed a cross section of the Lemba Tribe and the Y chromosome passed on by many males in the population proved to contain the Cohen Modal Haplotype (CMH). Among Jews the CMH marker is most prevalent among Cohanim or hereditary priests. In addition, this marker is one that only emanates from the Middle East and is not found in any identifiable African Roots. Even more astounding are the following stats: The CMH markers show up in fifty percent of the Lemba tested. The same marker shows up only three to five percent of the time in the general Jewish population."

6

Tamar

Standing Forth, Ascending, High, Lofty, Erect, Upright, and Palm Tree.

The sons of Judah; Er, and Onan, and Shelah: which three were born unto him of the daughter of Shua the Canaanitess. And Er, the firstborn of Judah, was evil in the sight of the LORD; and he slew him.

And Tamar his daughter in law bore him Pharez and Zerah. All the sons of Judah were five.
1 Chronicles 2:3-4

Since Abraham is the first man the Scriptures named a Hebrew, all of his offspring would be considered Hebrew also. We have proven that his Hebrew bloodline began with Ishmael whose mother was an Egyptian African named Hagar. We witnessed that Ishmael married an Egyptian African and produced the twelve princes of the Ishmaelites. We have discussed Abraham's third wife, another African named Keturah, who had six more sons to continue the Hebrew ancestry which included Midian, the Father of the Midianites who has a very important history among the children of Israel. This means outside of the twelve Tribes of Israel, there are many other tribes that became nations who are also Hebrew. The only other offspring of Abraham who would continue the Hebrew bloodline is the promised seed of Isaac. Isaac's mother, Sarah, was not African.

At this point, you could say my premise that Black Wives are the mother of all Hebrew people is not founded in truth. Not so fast. Sarah was not African, but the twelve Tribes of Israel did not come from Isaac. They came from Jacob and each of Jacob's sons married African women who mothered the children of each of the twelve Tribes. Therefore, Black women are the mothers of all Hebrew people. The next Black Wife that Matters in Scripture is the wife of Jacob's fourth son, Judah. Elohim did not see fit to include her name but instead simply stated:

And Judah saw there a daughter of a certain Canaanite, whose name was Shuah; and he took her, and went in unto her. Genesis 38:2

We know Judah married this Canaanite woman who was the daughter of a Canaanite man named Shuah because Genesis 38:12 says, *"And in the process of time the daughter of Shuah Judah's wife died . . ."* Judah stands out among the twelve sons of Jacob because his tribe was designated by Yehovah as the royal seed, those who would reign as king and produce the King of kings and Lord of lords. Therefore, Yehovah took great concern as to what took place with Judah and his sons. Unfortunately, things did not fare too well early on in the young prince's life. Immediately after Judah and his brethren sold their youngest brother Joseph to a caravan of Ishmaelites, who then sold him into Egypt, Judah strayed away from the household. Judah was the one who did not want to kill Joseph and recommended that they pull him out of the pit and sell him to the traveling merchantmen. His story picks up here:

And it came to pass at that time, that Judah went down from his brethren, and turned in to a certain Adullamite, whose name was Hirah.

And Judah saw there a daughter of a certain Canaanite, whose name was Shuah; and he took her, and went in unto her.

And she conceived, and bare a son; and he called his name Er.

And she conceived again, and bare a son; and she called his name Onan.

And she yet again conceived, and bare a son; and called his name Shelah: and he was at Chezib, when she bare him. Genesis 38:1-5

In an attempt to work through the trauma of what he did to his youngest brother, Judah declared his independence and attempted to spread his wings among the Canaanites. He became friends with an important brother name Hirah. Hirah means *pure, noble, highborn, splendid, distinguished, freedom,* and *liberty*.[28] Hirah was an *Adullamite* which means *justice of the people, and equity of the people*.[29] It seems Judah's crossroads led him to an association with nobility, distinguished, and liberty among the highborn folk who were about justice and equity of the people. What he really befriended was the walking manifestation of the "Woke" crowd. This is exactly what we are witnessing among the so-called elite of our day: "Wokeness." These elite hypocrites who preach and push "justice" and "equity" for the people live in gated communities with personal security far away from the actual effects of society.

In Judah's season of exploration, he marries a Canaanite woman whose father's name was Shuah. *Shuah* means *a sinking down (as in the mud), settling down, bowed down (the mind or soul), despair, depressed,* and *pit*.[30] The one whose bloodline would birth the Lion from the Tribe of Judah has separated himself from his brethren and found himself sinking down in the mud with his mind and soul bowed down and in a state of despair and depression. The pit that he colluded with his brothers to throw Joseph in, he now experiences in his own heart. How prophetic this story is of our times. The "woke" and elite who say they are for "justice" and "equity" are actually sinking down in the mud, full of despair and depression.

Judah marries an African Canaanite woman and has three sons by her. Something remarkably interesting occurs in the life of Judah's sons. The first two are killed by Yahweh. You do not find this too often in Scripture. First of all, Yahweh took personal interest in the posterity of Judah for reasons aforementioned. As always, the enemy understands the power and purpose of those who carry great destiny and attempts to infiltrate them and spoil the plans early on. Judah knew he was important, but to what extent? The Scriptures do not inform us exactly what the two elder sons of Judah did to exact Divine judgment. Genesis 38:7 says:

And Er, Judah's firstborn, was wicked in the sight of the LORD; and the LORD slew him.

Er means *awake, watchful, alert,* and *watchman*.[31] Evidently, he was awake, watchful and alert to some very wicked behavior. Obviously, anyone in Judah's lineage would be fallen and sinful, but there were certain demonic strongholds Yehovah did not want in the Royal Seed Bloodline. If we check the Answer Key of Genesis ten, it will shed some insight:

And the border of the Canaanites was from Sidon, as thou comest to Gerar, unto Gaza; as thou goest, unto Sodom, and Gomorrah . . ." Genesis 10:19

The wicked cities of Sodom and Gomorrah were actually in the territory of the Canaanites. This means the abomination of sodomy was in practice within certain Canaanite tribes. I believe Er, whose mom was a Canaanite, and who was born in the land of Canaan, participated in sodomy. If it is in the root, it is in the fruit. It was Canaan who sodomized his grandfather Noah and caused Noah to curse him and his descendants. This is part of the reason Abraham and Isaac did not want their sons marrying Canaanite women (as well as the polytheism). We witness this spirit at work today in the Church and specifically the Black church. *Judah* means *praise* and no other people group praise Yahweh like His Black people.[32] The Black agenda in America became the LGBTQ movement and we could not really explain how. Now we know. But the enemy knows if he can get that demonic spirit of sodomy back in the family of Judah (*praise*), it will bring Yahweh's judgment once again. Black people created the extremely popular genre called Gospel music. Sodomites run this industry, and it is not a coincidence that the godfather of Gospel music, James Cleveland, was also a sodomite. This is exactly what parts of the Black church is experiencing as sodomites have become a part of the culture. Instead of there being repentance and a turning away from this wickedness, it has become normal and accepted. Certain major Black denominations have witnessed Yahweh judging those who participate in this wickedness without repentance.

Before Er's death, Judah chose a Canaanite wife for him named Tamar. Genesis 38:6 says, "And Judah took a wife for Er his firstborn, whose name was Tamar." After God killed Er,

Judah's second son, Onan was instructed to take Er's wife, Tamar, and raise up seed in order for his brother's name to continue. However, Onan did not do this, rather, he enjoyed having physical intimacy with Tamar then spilled his seed on the floor, intentionally denying her a son to perpetuate the bloodline. *Onan* means *able bodied, strong, stout, virile,* and *vigorous.*[33] With all of Onan's vigor and virility, he refused to use it for the purposes of Yahweh. Genesis 38:10 says, "And the thing which he did displeased the LORD: wherefore he slew him also." The beginning of Judah's family is quite horrific, and unfortunately it gets worse.

Signet, Bracelet & Staff

The name *Tamar* means *palm tree, upright, standing forth,* and *ascending.*[34] Judah chose Tamar for his eldest son, but Judah did not do right by her. Judah promised his youngest son, Shelah, to her, once Shelah became of age. However, he forfeited on this promise once Shelah was old enough. Tamar felt slighted for this. She had a sense of destiny even though Judah and his sons did not. This radiant African regent set out to do whatever was necessary to set things in order and continue the Royal Family's Bloodline. The only upright one who had character in this tragic story was Tamar. She would be the one to preserve the Tribe of Judah.

Tamar veiled her face, covered her body, and sat out in the open. Judah thought her to be a harlot and propositioned her. She asked him for a pledge in return for allowing Judah to lay with her and he agreed. Tamar asked for Judah's signet, bracelet, and staff. After Judah laid with his daughter-in-law (that he thought was a harlot), she conceived. Judah sent Tamar payment, a young goat by his friend the Adullamite, but she was nowhere to be found. After three months, word got back to Judah that his daughter-in-law had played the harlot and was pregnant. Tamar was brought before Judah and said:

By the man, whose these are, am I with child: and she said, Discern, I pray thee, whose are these, the signet, and bracelets, and staff.

And Judah acknowledged them, and said, She hath been more righteous than I; because that I gave her not to Shelah my son. And he knew her again no more.
Genesis 38:25-26

Tamar resorted to deception in order to continue the Royal Bloodline. The same man who chose her for his eldest son, ended up being the one who impregnated her. Tamar gave birth to twin sons: Pharez and Zarah. This young Black woman is listed in the lineage of Jesus because she did what she had to do in order for Yahweh's Royal Line to endure. She persevered through the Divine judgment of her husband and brother-in-law and years of denial from Judah's youngest son, Shelah. Like the soul of every Black woman, before and after her, she kept the faith. Even when Judah didn't realize the power of his one destiny, this beautiful Black wife did because Black Wives Matter.

Tamar was wise enough to take the items from Judah that identified his authority and position in the kingdom. Judah was like many men of color today who carry Yahweh's signet, bracelets, and staff of authority, but can be found out in the streets laying with whores because they do not really understand who they are. I'm reminded of Saul when Prophet Samuel was searching for him to anoint him as the first king of Israel. Samuel found Saul out searching for his father's asses. Many of the world's poor and oppressed men are out searching for "asses" while Elohim is looking to give them the Kingdom. A signet is a seal officially used to give personal authority to a document in lieu of a signature. When Abraham's head servant Eliezar decided that Rebekah was the woman Isaac was supposed to marry, he gave her bracelets. These bracelets were a pre-engagement gift. Bracelets are worn on the wrists, so they are connected with our actions and choices. Wearing bracelets meant you were separated from your environment and preserved for a specific or even sacred purpose. Judah's bracelets symbolized his separation from his other brothers by Divine decree of his bloodline being that of kings. This was enforced by Yahweh as Judah's first two sons were killed.

The staff of Judah signified guidance as a shepherd. Judah was a shepherd by trade and his staff was an important tool. It was a walking stick in the daily life of a shepherd. It signified power because it supports the hand and arm and through it the whole body. Moses stretched forth his staff (rod) preceding the miracles of Yahweh. Therefore, the staff represents power. When Tamar requested Judah's signet, bracelets, and staff before Judah could lay with her, she was receiving the spiritual, moral, and generational right to raise seed for the Most High. Her name means *palm tree*, and *upright*.[35] She did not go to these lengths for selfish or carnal reasons, but this Black woman of destiny had better discernment than the progenitor of the future Tribe of Judah. She had the urgency and integrity necessary to establish the heritage of the Royal Line. The enemy fought tenaciously at the genesis of Judah's life to throw a wrench in God's plan to establish the Royal Lineage for the coming Messiah because he remembered well the prophesy of Genesis 3:15:

And I will put enmity between thee and the woman, and between thy seed and her seed; it shall bruise thy head, and thou shalt bruise his heel.

Tamar understood the risk of her insidious plan to become pregnant by her father-in-law, but destiny protected her. She took from Judah all the evidence needed to acquit her once she was revealed to be with child. She possessed the royal seal (signet), the royal covenant (bracelets), and the royal power (staff). Maybe Judah's wife's name was never recorded because Yehovah knew it would be Tamar who kept the posterity of the Royal Bloodline.

The Black Presence in the Bible Quote: Pages 126-128

"It is acceptable by both biblical and non-biblical scholars that Hamitic peoples (descendants of Noah's son Ham) are the ancestors and originators of an explicit line of Black/African peoples all over the earth. Ham became the father of Cush, Egypt, Put, and Canaan, all Black descendants of their Black father.

At this point we are now in a position to further appreciate the Black ancestry of Christ. This information is anchored in the genealogical table of Matthew, and, in this particular approach, and to the surprise of some, it concerns no less that three of the four women are noted as being ancestors of the Lord!

The first woman is mentioned in Matthew 1:3 and is named Tamar. The Story of Tamar can be found in Genesis 38. Tamar was known to be a Canaanite woman by virtue of her implied identification as a Canaanitess, and where she dwelt, in a city called Timnath. Timnath was in the vicinity of Adullam, a known Canaanite town (cf. 38:1,2,6,11,13). Tamar became an ancestor of Christ Jesus through a child she mothered by her own father-in-law Judah. The child's name was Perez (Matthew 1:3).

The second woman is mentioned in Matthew 1:5 and is named Rahab. The story of Rahab is found in Joshua 2:1-21 and 6:17-25. Rahab was known to be a Canaanite, an inhabitant of the city of Jericho. She was the prostitute who helped the two Israelite spies when they surveyed the land of Canaan. As a result of her actions of faith, the lives of Rahab and her household were spared during the Israelite conquest of Jericho (cf. Hebrews 11:31 and James 2:25). It was an ancestor of Christ Jesus named Boaz who was in fact the son of Rahab, the Canaanite (Matthew 1:5).

The third woman who was a Black ancestor of Christ Jesus is mentioned in Matthew 1:6 as the "wife of Uriah," Bathsheba by name. The Story of Bathsheba is recorded in 2 Samuel 11. This is most known as the Story of David and Bathsheba. What is often overlooked is the fact that Bathsheba was married to Uriah the Hittite. It is widely known and accepted that the Hittites were a Hamitic people. They descended from Heth, a son of Canaan (Genesis 10:15 and 23:10). If in fact Bathsheba shared the same ethnic origin as her husband (a reasonable assumption), then the child born to her and David, Solomon by name, did indeed have Black ancestry in his veins. Solomon was an ancestor of Christ Jesus (Matthew 1:6).

Immediately the objection may be raised: But Joseph, whose genealogy is recorded in Matthew's Gospel, had nothing to do with the birth of Jesus, for Jesus was miraculously conceived and born to a woman who was a virgin. Joseph's seed had nothing to do with the humanity of Jesus. Thus, any reference to Black African blood in the genealogical line of Jesus through Joseph is invalid!

Such an objection would be devastating to our argument, save for one bit of enlightening information. It is virtually without disagreement among biblical scholars that Mary as well as Joseph was "of the house of David" (Luke 1:27 and Luke 2:4). This blood relation of Mary to her forefather King David is corroborated by other Scriptures (see Luke 1:32, 69; Matthew 9:27; 15:22; 20:30, 31; Mark 10:47, 48).

Therefore Mary, as the woman who physically mothered Christ, was of David's line and is foreshadowed in the prophecies that the promised Messiah was to be the very offspring of David as well as successor to the Davidic throne (cf. 2 Samuel 7:12; 1 Kings 8:25-26; Isaiah 7:13-14, 9:7; Jeremiah 23:5, 33:15, 17; John 7:42 and Mark 11:10). The Apostle Paul wrote that "Jesus Christ . . . was a descendent from David" (2 Timothy 2:8), and furthermore states that Jesus Christ "was made of the seed of David according to the flesh." (Romans 1:3). Indeed, according to His own testimony, Christ Jesus Himself is both "the root and the offspring of David" (Revelation 22:16).

Now insomuch as the references to women of Hamitic descent, their impact upon the House of David, (Jesus' lineage) is so affected by virtue of Mary, His mother. This is true in both the cases of Tamar and Rahab, for they preceded David and his house. Further, it may not be unreasonable to assume that Mary's bloodline may also have been influenced through Solomon, the son of Bathsheba and David. The fact that Luke's Gospel carries a heightened emphasis on the physical descent of Christ gives an added strength to this argument.

So, we have it. Tamar, Rahab, and Bathsheba, each of Hamitic descent, each a lineal ancestor of Christ Jesus according to reliable genealogical information from Matthew's and Luke's Gospel. Ontologically and genealogically speaking, Jesus is Black, for Black ancestral blood ran in His human veins."[36]

7

Wives of Jacob's Sons

And they slew Hamor and Shechem his son with the edge of the sword, and took Dinah out of Shechem's house, and went out.

They took their sheep, and their oxen, and their asses, and that which was in the city, and that which was in the field.

And all their wealth, and all their little ones, and their wives took they captive, and spoiled even all that was in their house.
Genesis 34:26, 28-29

Some Bible scholars believe the same year that Joseph was sold into slavery, and Judah married a Canaanite, the daughter of Shuah, that the other sons of Jacob were married also. Genesis 46: 10 says ". . . and Shaul the son of a Canaanitish woman." The book, *Legend of the Jews*, states that Reuben married a Canaanite woman named Elyoram, daughter of Uzzi of Timnath.[37] Asher's first wife was Adon, the daughter of Ephlal, a grandson of Ishmael.[38] Zebulon's wife was Maroshah, the daughter of Molad, a grandson of Midian, the son of Abraham and Keturah.[39] Benjamin married Arbat, the daughter of Zimran, a son of Abraham and Keturah.[40] The forty-sixth chapter of Genesis records the names of Jacob's grandsons and the only mother listed is the mother of Simeon's son Shual, who was a Canaanitish woman.

The Book of Jasher, chapter forty-five, states that Reuben's wife was Eliuram, the daughter of Avi the Canaanite (of Timnah).[41] It records that Zebulun went to Midian and married Merishah the daughter of Molad, the son of Abida, the son of Midian.[42] Non-biblical sources state that four of Jacob's sons (Reuben, Asher, Zebulon, and Benjamin) married African women and had sons. Of course, this does not include Simeon, Judah, and Joseph, which the Scriptures record married African woman and had sons. If we stop right here, we can safely state that seven out of Jacob's twelve sons married African wives and had sons who would now be considered African. This means more than half of the Tribes of Israel originated with African in their bloodline. Abraham, Isaac, and Jacob were in an African land with African allies and enemies and was promised an African territory by Yehovah. This is the truth that

European leaders in the Church have conveniently left out after many years of seminary study and teachings. There can only be one reason for this: White Supremacy!

If we allow ourselves to be put in the time and culture of these biblical days, it is easy to understand how these amazing African women were very open to intermarry the descendants of Shem. One of the reasons was because they were also people of color. The second reason was because Abraham, Isaac, and Jacob were very rich men. I'm not saying the African women were "gold diggers," but they were not messing with "no broke ninjas." The land of Canaan was breathtaking and so were the people.

Took by Possession

Besides Judah, Simeon, and Joseph, the Bible does not explicitly state that Jacob's other sons married African women or had children by them, but the Scripture does implicitly state it. The thirty-fourth chapter of Genesis tells the story of how a Black man name Shechem, the son of Hamor the Hivite, was the prince of the area named after him: Shechem, and how he raped Jacob's daughter, Dinah. His father, Hamor, entreated Jacob for Dinah's hand in marriage to Shechem after he raped her. Something interesting is stated concerning this defilement. Genesis 34:3 says:

And his soul clave unto Dinah the daughter of Jacob, and he loved the damsel, and spake kindly unto the damsel.

This is proof of how twisted someone's definition of love can be. Shechem's soul was bound to the woman he raped, and the Scriptures say that he loved her and spoke kindly to her. This is absolutely demented. Whenever sex is involved, whether permitted or not, a soul-tie (feeling bound to the person) is activated. Shechem actually began to be nice towards Dinah and desired to marry her after forcing himself sexually upon her. He even had his father approach Dinah's father, Jacob, about receiving her hand in marriage. Once Dinah's brothers found out that Shechem raped their sister, Simeon and Levi took matters in their own hands. They falsely agreed to Shechem and Dinah's marriage on one condition: that all the men under Hamor's authority in the town would adhere to the Israelites' custom of circumcision. After Hamor and Shechem agreed and were circumcised and all the men of the city were circumcised, Simeon and Levi waited until the third day. Then, when the circumcised men would be the most sensitive, Simeon and Levi overpowered and murdered them. What occurs next is the proof that all of Jacob's sons had African wives. Genesis 34:28-29 says:

They took their sheep, and their oxen, and their asses, and that which was in the city, and that which was in the field,

And all their wealth, and all their little ones, and their wives took they captive, and spoiled even all that was in the house.

Simeon and Levi destroyed Hamor, Shechem, and all the males. At this point, they controlled the city, so they went ahead and completely spoiled it and part of the spoils were all the wives and daughters of the men they just murdered. I believe Scripture does not list the wives of many of the sons of Jacob because when we know details like this concerning the life of Jacob's sons, we can connect the dots. Simeon and Levi reported the great spoils to their father Jacob, and their brothers. Jacob feared the rest of the Canaanite tribes would retaliate. But the Scripture is clear, Simeon and Levi took many African widows and their daughters back home with them. These beautiful Black women would become wives and handmaidens for the rest of Jacob's sons. Jacob and his sons not only sojourned in the Black land of Ham's fourth son, Canaan, but they all married Black women and procreated with Black women which means that every single Tribe of Israel began with Black offspring. Even if you incorrectly believe that Abraham, Isaac, and Jacob were White (which is impossible because they were not from Japheth, but Shem), it is a fact that each son of Jacob married a Black woman. These Black women mothered the Tribes of Israel and there is no doubt that African blood is in each tribe and was there from the very beginning. Yahweh saw to it that His amazing Black daughters mothered His chosen people tribes and there could be no greater proof that Black Wives Matter!

Let's not forget how many times the children of Israel would mix with other tribes and nations. Elohim never intended for Israel to be a master race or superior to any other people group. He knew they would fall, fail, sin, and show themselves unworthy of His love and mercy time and time again. He did not choose them based on their righteousness, but on His own righteousness. If God didn't want the world to believe His chosen people were Black, why did He allow them to repeatedly marry African women and give them an African territory called Canaan Land?

Mixed Multitude

Besides Black women giving birth to the beginning of the twelve Tribes of Israel, Jacob, his sons, and all their families relocated to Egypt under the protection of Joseph, Egypt's Prince. After hundreds of years of enslavement by the Egyptians, Exodus 12:38 says:

And a mixed multitude went up also with them, and flocks, and herds, even very much cattle.

A mixed multitude left with the children of Israel. They were not the children of Israel, but a separate group. Common sense and history inform us that any people enslaved by another nation for hundreds of years will also mix together. The African Americans alive today in America do not look like their forefathers who were originally sold into slavery in America because there has been a lot of mixing of the races since 1619. Egypt is an African country, and it is easy to understand there was some mixing of the children of Israel with the Egyptian Africans. I can't imagine the children of Israel becoming lighter during their time in Egypt, but I can imagine them becoming darker. But this mixed multitude was separate from the already mixed Israelites in Egypt. *Mixed* is the Hebrew word *ereb* meaning *mingled, woof (woven fabric)* and *interwoven*[43] Some Rabbis believe the mixed multitude were Egyptians who converted to the Hebrew religion. This is similar to the Gentiles who believe in Christ and are grafted into the Body of Christ. This mixed multitude were interwoven into the children of Israel. They were mentioned again as they incited the Israelites to sin. Numbers 11:4-5 records:

And the mixed multitude that was among them fell a lusting: and the children of Israel also wept again, and said, Who shall give us flesh to eat?

We remember the fish, which we did eat in Egypt freely; the cucumbers, and the melons, and the leeks and the onions, and the garlick.

Some of the mixed multitude may have begun in Pharoah's house. Exodus 9:20 says, *"He that feared the word of the Lord among the servants of Pharaoh made his servants and his cattle flee into the houses."* What's not widely understood is that many Israelites did not depart during the Exodus and many Egyptians did. The application of the blood of lambs or goats on the doorposts the night of Passover was purely voluntary, and it was open and optional for any household in Egypt who wanted to participate. Shortly after the death of Joshua, Judges 3:5-6 says:

And the children of Israel dwelt among the Canaanites, Hittites, and Amorites, and Perizzites, and Hivites, and Jebusites.

Black Wives Matter

And they took their daughters to be their wives, and gave their daughters to their sons, and served their gods.

8

Asenath

Dedicated to Neith

And Pharoah called Joseph's name Zaphnathpaaneah; and he gave him to wife Asenath the daughter of Potipherah priest of On. And Joseph went out over all the land of Egypt.
Genesis 41:45

Black Wives Matter

The last of Jacob's sons to get married was Joseph because he was sold into slavery in Egypt. At the age of thirty, he was exalted to second in command in Egypt, only behind Pharaoh himself. Pharoah awarded Joseph a wife named Asenath, the daughter of the priest of On. Asenath or Asnat means *dedicated to Neith*.[44] Neith was the Egyptian goddess of the cosmos, fate, wisdom, waters, mothers, and childbirth.[45] Jacob and his sons lived among Africans, in an African land, and now Joseph is in another African country and married to an African woman from the African country where he lived.

This is just the tip of the iceberg. There is still Zipporah, Bathsheba, Queen of Sheba, and many more to come. For the average African American Believer in Christ to be ignorant about the mountain of Black History plainly written in Scripture shows what a great job the European Church leaders have done to hide Black History and how poor of a job Black clergy have done to teach it.

There is an awesome relationship with Black priests and their daughters marrying great men within the Tribes of Israel. Joseph married Asenath, the priest of On. Moses married Zipporah, the daughter of Jethro, the priest of Midian. Aaron's son Eleazer (one of the first priests of Israel), married another daughter of Jethro, the priest of Midian. Yehovah was revealing to us how the Black man isn't only a part of the twelve Tribes of Israel, but he is also intimately connected to Yahweh's Priesthood. This will be discussed later concerning the Bantu and Libre Tribes.

After Joseph's brothers sold him to the Ishmaelites, they took Joseph to Egypt and sold him to Potiphar. Joseph was seventeen at the time. He did not become the Viceroy of Egypt until he was thirty. Therefore, Joseph spent thirteen years as the property of others. Once he was exalted, there was a great famine throughout the Earth. However, Yahweh had already given Joseph the wisdom to not only survive the famine but to excel during the famine and it came by way of his interpretation of Pharaoh's dream. Yahweh had Joseph store up corn and grain during the seven years of plenty that preceded the seven years of famine. This foreknowledge caused Pharaoh to become one of the largest property owners in the world. Since the famine was so grievous, tribes and nations came to Egypt for grain and ended up bartering all of their cattle and real estate. By the end of the famine, Pharaoh owned all the land in Egypt and Canaan.

Tribe of Ephraim

Joseph did not "stand out like a sore thumb" in Egypt because he was a man of color also. When he married an Egyptian woman, their children would of course, be Black. Therefore, the two sons of Joseph, Ephraim and Manasseh were Black Tribes. Reuben forfeited his tribal birthright by laying with his father Jacob's handmaiden (Genesis 49:4-5). The two sons of Joseph took Joseph's place among the tribes (there is no Tribe of Joseph) and would later replace Reuben. After Joseph died, another Pharoah came into power who did not know Joseph and since the children of Israel did not return to the land of Canaan, but remained in Egypt, they began worshipping false gods (Ezekiel 20:7-8). Therefore, Yehovah allowed them to be enslaved by Pharoah. At the end of the 430 years (that Yahweh prophesied was coming to an end) Yahweh raised up Moses to be Israel's deliverer.

We are very familiar with Joshua who was Moses' minister. Did you know that Joshua was Black? As a matter of fact, the only two men who came back with a good report from spying out Canaan Land (Joshua and Caleb) were Black men. Numbers 11:28 says, *"And Joshua the son of Nun, the servant of Moses . . ."* 1 Chronicles 7:20-27 gives the lineage of Ephraim, and Joshua (Jehoshuah) is a descendant of Ephraim which means he was a Black man since Ephraim and Manasseh were the offspring of Joseph and his Egyptian wife. Joseph's bloodline that's connected to the twelve Tribes of Israel was designated to be mothered by an African. This makes their descendants Black. The twelve Tribes' African wives and mothers were all Hebrew. Remember, Hebrews are anyone from the bloodline of Abraham. Israelites are any descendants of the twelve Tribes of Israel, and Jews are only direct descendants of the Tribe of Judah. God's chosen people have been a mixed people from the very beginning with one hundred percent African people. The nation of Israel and Jewish people should not even be mentioned today without the recognition of their Blackness.

Caleb, the Son of Jephunneh

One of the most diverse Tribes of Israel is the Tribe of Judah; the Tribe of the Royal Bloodline in which our Savior would come from. A very important man emerges within this tribe named Caleb. Caleb was a leader among the tribes after the exodus from Egyptian slavery. He and Joshua were the only two people of their generation who did not die in the wilderness and went into the Promised Land of Canaan. Numbers 32:12 states that Caleb is a Kenezite (Kenizzite):

Save Caleb the son of Jephunneh the Kenezite, and Joshua the son of Nun: for they have wholly followed the Lord.

God originally promised the land of Canaan to Abraham's seed after the sins of the Amorites were full. One of the Canaanite tribes listed are the Kenizzites. Genesis 15:18-19 says *"The Kenites, and the Kenizzites, and the Kadmonites."* From this we can see that Caleb who is listed as a Kenizzite is a Canaanite and that makes him African. However, Numbers 13:6 says that Caleb was from the Tribe of Judah. Something unique happened in the Tribe of Judah that did not occur in other tribes. Judah was more inclusive and engrafted other tribes or families within their tribe. This made them one of the largest tribes numbered during a census. This is sort of like the Gentiles who are engrafted into the Body of Christ because of Israel's rejection of Yeshua; the Kenizzites and others were engrafted into the Tribe of Judah. They could have integrated into the Tribe of Judah (converted to their faith) before Israel's enslavement to Egypt, similar to Ruth, the Moabitess and

Rahab, the harlot of Jericho. Maybe it was just Caleb's family who chose to follow Yahweh, and not groups of people of the Kenizzite Tribe.

Nonetheless, Caleb rose to prominence in Israel because of his heart toward the Most High. He was chosen to represent the Tribe of Judah as one of the twelve spies (one from each tribe) to search out Canaan Land. Only he and Joshua returned from their mission with a good report. The other ten spies gave a report of fear and terror of the giants in the land of Canaan. Their words of doubt and unbelief spread throughout the camp, and this was one of the many reasons why God refused to let them go into the Promised Land.

9

Zipporah

Little Bird, Sparrow, Chirper, and Twitterer

Now the priest of Midian had seven daughters: and they came and drew water, and filled the troughs to water their father's flock.

And the shepherds came and drove them away: but Moses stood up and helped them, and watered their flock.

And when they came to Reuel their father, he said, How is it that ye are come so soon to day?

And they said, An Egyptian delivered us out of the hand of the shepherds, and also drew water enough for us, and watered the flock.

And he said unto his daughters, And where is he? why is it that ye have left the man? call him, that he may eat bread.

And Moses was content to dwell with the man: and he gave Moses Zipporah his daughter. Exodus 2:16-21

Abortion

The story of Moses began during a royal decree from Pharaoh to legalize the murder of all newborn Israelite males. When Moses was born, his mother made a small ark from bushes and slime and placed Moses in it and sent Moses up the Nile River. The daughter of Pharaoh saw him and had her servants bring the baby to her and she became Moses' mother. Even if sin is legalized by government, it is still sin. Whether or not it is homosexual "marriages" or abortion, if God is against it, it is sin. I am baffled at the idiotic lengths the "Woke" mob of today take to normalize sin. They begin by creating stupid words for their demonic deeds like abortion. Abortion does not sound as evil and cruel as the murder of life in the womb, does it? "Woke" is the American left ideas involving identity politics and social justice. The phrase "stay woke" started with African American activists to raise awareness about police shootings of African Americans. The corrupt, rich, fools of today who call themselves "Elite" stole this terminology, and the phrase is now mostly associated with their pathetic ideology. Take for example, Planned Parenthood. Who would think to call the slaughterhouses of the unborn, Planned Parenthood? Only "Woke" people would name it Planned Parenthood. How are you planning for parenthood by doing the very thing that eliminates you from being a parent? Who would think the proper way to correct or reform the injustices of minorities in the criminal justice system would be to give criminals no bail and have most non-violent felony crimes not charged and released immediately? Only "Woke" folk would think to do that. Who would think it is okay to segregate grade school classrooms and teach all the white children that they are oppressors? Only "Woke" people would think to do that.

The only way Black Wives can Matter is if she gives birth and nurtures the next generation. A Black wife cannot do that if she is murdering her own children. This is the reason satan has targeted the Black woman so fiercely, because he knows she gave birth to humanity and Yahweh entrusted her to give birth to all of His Hebrew people. Every tribe, color, and race came from her. She is the original woman (womb-man), and the enemy knows if there is a Genesis, there will be a Revelation. The Black woman was at the beginning and Yehovah will use her in the end. African American women represent 12.6% of the population.[46] However, they account for 38.4% percent of all murders of life in the womb in America.[47] This is not by accident. In some places, like New York, Black women murder more life in the womb in a year than they give birth to life in the womb in a year.[48] We have to do better at reminding Black women of her awesome history in the world, and her value in the Eyes of Christ.

Shiphrah & Puah

Pharaoh commanded all the Egyptian midwives to kill all the Hebrew male babies as they were born. There were two particular midwives who must have been the most experienced, whose names were Shiphrah and Puah. *Shiphrah* means *bright, shining, splendid, polished,* and *beautiful.*[49] *Puah* means *mouth, orifice, blast, utterance,* and *command.*[50] When it comes to government sanctioning the murder of life in the womb, Elohim will have Shiphrahs and Puahs in position to be His Mouth to utter and command justice and save the lives of the innocent who will be our next generation and will be bright, shining, and beautiful. These two midwives feared Yahweh and refused to murder the Hebrew male seed. God blessed them for preserving life in the womb and gave them families of their own. As a reward for saving the physical bodies (house) of His chosen people, Yehovah made them their own house. We are all called to be present-day Shiphrahs and Puahs and speak against the murder of innocent life in the womb so that the righteousness of Yahweh will shine brightly in our nation.

Moses' Mother

Exodus 2:1 introduces the father and mother of Moses: "And there went a man of the house of Levi, and took to wife a daughter of Levi." Moses' father's name and his mother's name are not mentioned here. It simply says that both were from the Tribe of Levi. Although Israel was enslaved to Egypt, it was different from African American slavery in America. The children of Israel remained in the Land of Goshen during the entirety of their bondage, and they married as they pleased. But the sixth chapter of Exodus gives us more detailed information concerning Aaron's and Moses' parents.

And Amram took him Jochebed his father's sister to wife; and she bare him Aaron and Moses: and the years of life of Amram were an hundred and thirty and seven years. Exodus 6:20

This passage reveals that Aaron's and Moses' father's name was Amram and their mother's name was Jochebed, and she was actually their great aunt because she was Amram's father's sister. It seems the enemy discerned the coming of a great deliverer in Israel, so he had Pharaoh proclaim the death of all baby boys born of Hebrew women. As Moses' mother, Jochebed, wittingly maneuvered around the certain execution of her son, Yahweh's Hand was not finished concerning Moses.

Who would Pharaoh's daughter get to nurse Moses? As Yehovah would have it, Moses' sister was one of Pharaoh's servants and she recommended her own mother to nurse Moses. Moses was actually raised by his own mother until he was a teenager. When Moses was about the age of forty, he witnessed an Egyptian slave master abusing a Hebrew slave and Moses murdered the Egyptian. Once word got to Pharaoh of what Moses did, Moses fled into the wilderness for his life. This is when he came across the women at the well in Midian.

Moses was on foot and traveled to the Land of Midian. We have already proven that Midian was one of the six Black Hebrew sons of Abraham and Keturah. Moses now finds himself in the Land of Midian among this Black tribe of people who are actually his blood cousins. He stumbled upon the daughters of Reuel attempting to water their father's flock at a well. Shepherding was not an occupation that most wanted, and it usually fell upon the lowest ranked family member in the home. If a household had all sons, the youngest son would be appointed the task as we see in the Story of David, the youngest of eight sons. There were times where this job fell upon the daughters, as in the case of Rebekah. Abraham sent his head servant, Eliezer, to find a bride for his son Isaac. Eliezer found Rebekah, just like Moses found Zipporah, at a well watering her father's flock. These shepherdesses proved to be extraordinary women and wives to their husbands.

Zipporah's father has many names in Scripture. He is introduced as Reuel in Exodus chapter two, but he is most known by the name, Jethro. Exodus 3:1 says, *"Now Moses kept the flock of Jethro his father in law, the priest of Midian . . ."* This Black man will prove to be one of the most influential men in Scripture. He was the priest of Midian and there is no evidence that he worshiped false gods. Jethro was a follower of Yahweh. As aforementioned, God chose Abraham because he knew that Abraham would teach his children in the way of Yehovah (Genesis 18:19). Because Abraham was faithful to teach his household concerning the ways of Yahweh, many of his descendants would naturally follow Yahweh. Midian was Abraham's fourth son by Keturah. Moses married a daughter of the priest of Midian. Jethro was not a priest of the false gods of the Canaanites, but he was a priest of the Most High. This is consequential because this would mean Jethro was a priest of Yehovah before Aaron and his sons became priests. Proof of this will be shown shortly. This would not be the first time this happened because Abraham met Melchizedek, the king and priest of Salem. Genesis 14:18-20 records:

And Melchizedek king of Salem brought forth bread and wine: and he was the priest of the most high God.

And he blessed him, and said, Blessed be Abram of the most high God, possessor of heaven and earth:

And blessed be the most high God, which hath delivered thine enemies into thy hand. And he gave him tithes of all.

Melchizedek was the king and priest of Salem. Salem is the ancient name of Jerusalem (Jeru-Salem). Jerusalem is located in the African Land of Canaan and the Canaanite Tribe of Jebusite originally inhabited this land. This means Melchizedek was a Black king and priest. Melchizedek was a king and priest of Yahweh generations before Yahweh established the Levitical priesthood through Aaron and his sons. This passage clearly presents Melchizedek greater than Abraham and states how Abraham paid Melchizedek tithes from the spoils of war. The book of Hebrews says that Abraham paid tithes to Melchizedek while the Levitical priesthood was still in Abraham's loins (Hebrews 7:10).

Pharoah had his own High Counsel, select men chosen to be King Pharoah's special counsel. Jethro sat on Pharoah's counsel but stepped down because he did not agree with the enslavement of the children of Israel. Besides disagreeing with slavery (of any kind), it is quite possible that Jethro also disagreed with Israel's enslavement in particular because he was a Hebrew, also, and he knew that the Israelites were his cousins and Yahweh's promised people.

Jethro's godly influence is revealed in his daughter Zipporah. The fourth chapter of Exodus records Moses and his family traveling from Midian to Egypt. Yahweh met Moses at an Inn and planned to kill him for not circumcising his son. Before the deliverer could deliver, he needed someone to deliver him and Moses' deliverer came by his wife, Zipporah. Zipporah discerned that her husband was in danger and quickly moved to protect her household by circumcising her son. Her actions saved Moses' life, but Zipporah was not pleased that she was put in that position. Therefore, she exclaimed, *"Surely a bloody husband art thou to me."* (Exodus 4:25) Moses would definitely testify that Black Wives Matter! Circumcision was instituted by Yehovah to Abraham as a token of His covenant with Abraham and his seed. How did Zipporah know about circumcision and how to actually perform the surgery? Her father Jethro who was the priest of Midian taught her. Jethro understood a great deal concerning the laws and ways of Yahweh and he would soon teach them to Moses.

Jethro's Names

Jethro is introduced in Scripture as Reuel and the name means *friend of God, shepherd of God,* and *led of God*.[51] The name *Jethro* means *His abundance, His superiority,* and *His excellence*.[52] Another name of Jethro is Hobab (Judges 4:11). *Hobab* means *beloved, cherished,* and *comforted*.[53] Numbers 10:29 calls him Raguel and it is the same as Reuel. Exodus 6:25 refers to him as *Putiel* which means *afflicted of God*.[54] I do not believe any other man in Scripture has these many names. This, in and of itself is profound because biblically, one must have an encounter with Elohim before a name change is granted. Moses' father-in-law had many encounters with

Elohim and many name changes. Abram waited twenty-five years for the promise of Isaac, and this is when he was given circumcision as the token of Yahweh's covenant and a name change was granted and he became Abraham. However, Jethro had several name changes which means his relationship with the Most High was extraordinary. Jethro was *a friend and shepherd of God*, *beloved and comforted*, and like Job, he was also *afflicted of God*. Have you ever noticed how the best singers never make it to celebrity status? Have you noticed how the best athletes never play professionally? And have you noticed that the best preachers are not known? The same is true in Scripture. Some of the greatest followers of Elohim are either not mentioned or we fail to recognize their greatness in the text. The same is true about David's famous Mighty Men. They were more exceptional warriors than David.

Moses' Mentor

The relationship between Moses and Jethro is a wonderful example of the power of mentoring. A mentor can only take you to the limits of where he himself has been. What was awesome for Moses was that Yehovah blessed him with a Black father-in-law whose leadership and character was so extensive that Moses would not exceed beyond him. Moses did not even realize his father-in-law's full potential as he spent forty years with him in the back of the desert in Midian. Jethro was meek and humble and played his cards close to his chest. I mean, Moses was the one hand picked by Elohim to be the Great Deliverer, right? Moses was the one who Yahweh would use to perform amazing miracles and punish the Egyptians, right?

Jethro is not recorded as being used by Yahweh to perform one miracle because he had no need to perform a miracle. He was assigned a greater responsibility and that was to mentor the miracle worker, help the Herculean Leader, teach the Titan of the Old Testament, and lead the Law Giver. Sometimes it is just wiser to play the backfield and let someone else take all the hits from being in the limelight. After Yahweh uses Moses to deliver the children of Israel from Egypt, Exodus 18:1,2,6 and 7 says:

When Jethro, the priest of Midian, Moses' father in law, heard of all that God had done for Moses, and for Israel his people, and that the LORD had brought Israel out of Egypt;

Then Jethro, Moses's father in law, took Zipporah, Moses' wife, after he had sent her back,

And he said unto Moses, I thy father in law Jethro am come unto thee, and thy wife, and her two sons with her.

And Moses went out to meet his father in law, and did obeisance, and kissed him; and they asked each other of their welfare; and they came into the tent.

Word of Elohim's great deliverance reached Jethro in Midian and he brought his daughter and her sons to Moses in the Sinai Desert. I would have loved to be a fly on the wall to hear Moses tell Jethro about all Yahweh had done for Israel to free them from Egypt. What a testimony! To understand the respect Moses had for his Black father-in-law, we read how

Moses made obeisance before him, even though Moses was raised in Pharoah's house. Moses was the one who led Israel out of Egypt by Yahweh's mighty Hand. This was Moses' hour! Yet, he still bowed down before the priest of Midian and everyone witnessed it.

Yahweh's Priest

And Jethro, Moses' father in law, took a burnt offering and sacrifices for God: and Aaron came, and all the elders of Israel, to eat bread with Moses' father in law before God.
Exodus 18:12

As aforementioned, Jethro was a priest of Yahweh before Aaron, and his sons were delivered from Egyptian captivity and established the Levitical priesthood. Aaron and his sons were ex-slaves who knew absolutely nothing about priestly ministry. But Elohim had an experienced priest close by to show them the way. Jethro wasn't just a priest of Midian, but he was The Priest of Midian. Moses' meeting with a group of women at a well in Midian would prove to be Divine destiny. The home he was invited to on that faithful evening would provide him a wife, children, extended family, and a father-in-law who would guide and assist him in leadership protocol that is realized in our lives even today. If Jethro were a pagan priest and attempted to offer up burnt offerings and sacrifices in the presence of Moses and Aaron, they would have immediately prohibited it. This is what Scripture refers to as "strange fire." And if Moses, Aaron, and the elders who attended this ceremony did not have the character to stop Jethro from performing such an abomination before Elohim, God Himself would have rendered instant judgment. However, this is not what occurred. All of the leaders of Israel attended this sacrificial ceremony before Yahweh and Jethro officiated it. Jethro's preeminence was revealed in this setting and there was no doubt that this Black man was a leader among leaders. The wisdom and assistance that Jethro provided Moses and Israel is seen even more as he observed Moses judge the people.

Jethro's Judicial Protocol

And it came to pass on the morrow, that Moses sat to judge the people: and the people stood by Moses from the morning unto the evening.

And when Moses' father in law saw all that he did to the people, he said, What is this thing that thou doest to the people? why sittest thou thyself alone, and all the people stand by thee from morning unto even?

And Moses said unto his father in law, Because the people come unto me to enquire of God.
Exodus 18:13-15

Jethro witnessed Moses wearing himself out by attempting to judge all of the children of Israel by himself. Yahweh had given Moses His Law and he thought since he was the only one who actually knew the Law, that he was responsible for judging it before the people. Jethro gives Moses excellent instructions concerning judging such a vast number of people.

And thou shalt teach them ordinances and laws, and shalt shew them the way wherein they must walk, and the work that they must do.

Moreover thou shalt provide out of all the people able men, such as fear God, men of truth, hating covetousness; and place such over them, to be rulers of thousands, and rulers of hundreds, rulers of fifties, and rulers of tens:

And let them judge the people at all seasons: and it shall be, that every great matter they shall bring unto thee, but every small matter they shall judge: so shall it be easier for thyself, and they shall bear the burden with thee.
Exodus 18:20-22

These instructions given to Moses by Jethro on proper protocol and structure in judicial matters has been used by many cultures since then. The Founding Fathers of America's Judicial System used Jethro's counsel to set up how America's Judicial Branch would be structured. In the United States, we have the Federal Court System, the State Court System, County Courts, and Municipal Courts. The Jewish Sanhedrin Counsel was established based on Jethro's advice and Jethro's bloodline was a part of its membership. Jethro is one of the most venerated men in all of Judaism, Orthodox and Babylonian, as a great sage and rabbi. The Druze religion regard Jethro as a prophet who communicated directly with God and related these Divine messages to Moses. Druze number about one million and pilgrimage annually between April 24th and April 28th to Hittin in lower Galilee to a holy shrine in order to commemorate the death of Jethro with open celebration.[55]

Hobab

Based on Numbers 10:29, the man named Hobab is Jethro's son, but Judges 4:11 makes it sound like Hobab is Moses' Father-in-law Jethro. Either way, Moses earnestly pleaded with Hobab to continue with Israel because they needed his expertise and his watchful eyes, as well as his discernment in the wilderness. Numbers 10:29-32 says:

And Moses said unto Hobab, the son of Raguel the Midianite, Moses' father in law, We are journeying unto the place of which the Lord said, I will give it you: come thou with us, and we will do thee good: for the Lord hath spoken good concerning Israel.

And he said unto him, I will not go; but I will depart to mine own land, and to my kindred.

And he said, Leave us not, I pray thee; forasmuch as thou knowest how we are to encamp in the wilderness, and thou mayest be to us instead of eyes.

And it shall be, if thou go with us, yea, it shall be, that what goodness the LORD shall do unto us, the same will we do unto thee.

Moses pleaded with Hobab to continue with Israel in their journeyings and reminded him about the blessings of Yehovah promised to Israel and how Israel would reward Hobab with the same inheritance. Hobab refused and Moses continued by stating, *"Leave us not, I pray thee . . ."* This was not some regular conversation with Moses' brother-in-law, but Yahweh's deliverer of Israel repeatedly implored Hobab to reconsider his position and worth in the children of Israel's journey. Moses began to prophesy to Hobab and told him he was "eyes" for Israel in the wilderness. What a petition Moses made. Unfortunately, Hobab declined. What Moses prophesied to Hobab 3,500 years ago, remains true today. *Hobab* which means *beloved, cherished,* and *comforted* is today's Black man.[56] We know about the difficulty and harshness of the wilderness environment. We understand lack, necessity, and how to survive off of little. It has been a long time since we ruled the world, but the first shall be last and the last shall be first. Yahweh is requiring our assistance once again. The Black man, Simon of Cyrene was compelled to help Yeshua carry His cross because Yeshua had been whipped and beaten beyond recognition and He could not see clearly because of all the blood and abuse Yeshua had endured. Once again, Elohim is calling for His Black man, His Hobabs, His *beloved* and *cherished,* to stand up in this hour and accept our Divine appointment with destiny and to be the "eyes" of the Body of Christ as we get closer to our Promised Land of the Lord's return.

10

Daughter of Putiel

And Eleazar Aaron's son took him one of the daughters of Putiel to wife; and she bare him Phinehas: these are the heads of the fathers of the Levites according to their families. Exodus 6:25

Elohim is finally about to establish His priesthood and the Tribe of Levi would be used exclusively for priests. Only Aaron and his sons are ordained of Yahweh to serve in the office and function of priests. The priesthood is important to the culture of Israel's livelihood because their existence is before the sacrifice of Yeshua, the Lamb of God. Therefore, a system was needed to temporarily cover their sins. Hebrews 9:22 instructs us:

And almost all things are by the law purged with blood; and without shedding of blood is no remission.

Aaron served as the first High Priest and his sons served as the first priests. Yahweh had the children of Israel build a Tabernacle, but it would be a mobile House of God because they were still migrating through the wilderness for forty years before they conquered Canaan Land. The generation of Israelites who were delivered from Egypt were a stiff-necked and rebellious people. They murmured, complained, and sought every occasion to defy Elohim. One of these times is recorded in Numbers twenty-five. The children of Israel committed whoredom with the daughters of Moab. They bowed down to the false god baalpeor, sacrificed unto him, and participated in open orgies with their temple whores. Yehovah instructed Moses to take all the leaders of the people who were involved and hang them before the Tabernacle. Then, He instructed all the judges to slay every person under their authority who participated in the idolatry. As this was all taking place, one of the men of Israel defiantly brought a Midianitish woman before Moses and the rest of the congregation and took her into a tent to have sex with her in in worship to baalpoer. This is when another unsung hero in Scripture stood up.

Phinehas

The Theological Wordbook of the Old Testament interprets *Phinehas* to mean *the bronze-colored one*.[57] The Egyptian use of the name means *the Black* or *the Nubian*.[58] The Hebrew meaning of *Phinehas* is *mouth of prophecy, mouth of brass, brazened faced,* and *bold-unabashed*.[59] Exodus 6:25 says that Aaron's son, Eleazar, married a daughter of Putiel and they had a son named Phinehas. Putiel happened to be another name for Moses' Father-in-law Jethro. Therefore, Moses was not the only Israelite who married one of Jethro's seven daughters. Aaron's son Eleazar also married one of Jethro's daughters. They should have had their own reality show called *Keeping Up With the Daughters of Jethro*. Phinehas was the recipient of a double portion priestly anointing because his mother was the daughter of Jethro, the Priest of Midian and his father was a priest and the son of Israel's first High Priest Aaron. Phinehas was also Hebrew from both parents' bloodline (Levi and Midian). Phinehas was a Black man and his name signified it: *the Black, the Nubian,* and *the bronze-colored one*. This Black man was a Levitical priest in Israel who witnessed the abomination and rebellion that broke out as the children of Israel began to worship baalpoer and engage in sinful idolatrous sexual worship to this false god. As Yahweh's Divine judgment was unleashed within the congregation of evil doers, the Scriptures say this about Phinehas:

And when Phinehas, the son of Eleazar, the son of Aaron the priest, saw it, he rose up from among the congregation, and took a javelin in his hand;

And he went after the man of Israel in the tent, and thrust both of them through, the man of Israel, and the woman through her belly. So the plague was stayed from the children of Israel.

And those that died in the plague were twenty and four thousand.
Numbers 25:7-9

Among all the congregation of Israel rose another hero for the ages. Phinehas was zealous for Yahweh and deeply offended at the open rebellion of the children of Israel. And when he saw the judgment of Yahweh destroying the people, his righteous indignation drove him to take matters into his own hands. He took a javelin and entered the tent of the boldest offender of Yahweh's Holiness, and he stuck both man and woman through and killed them while they were in the act of sexual worship to baalpoer. Elohim was so moved by this Black man's zeal for His Holiness that He stopped His Divine judgment where 24,000 of the children of Israel died. Yehovah spoke these words concerning Phinehas:

Phinehas, the son of Eleazar, the son of Aaron the priest, hath turned my wrath away from the children of Israel, while he was zealous for my sake among them, that I consumed not the children of Israel in my jealousy.

Wherefore say, Behold, I give unto him my covenant of peace:

And he shall have it, and his seed after him, even the covenant of an everlasting priesthood; because he was zealous for his God, and made an atonement for the children of Israel.
Numbers 25:11-13

Elohim declared something so awesome over Phinehas that is almost never seen in Scripture. He instantly established a covenant of peace and an everlasting priesthood with this young Black man and his seed forever. Let that sink in. Yahweh cannot lie. When He says something, it is settled! This means the everlasting priesthood He ordained with Phinehas and his seed cannot be altered no matter which priesthood is in operation throughout time. Glory! Where are the Phinehases of today? We are witnessing so much paganism and idolatry in the Body of Christ and we are all kings and priests of the Most High, yet many in the Church are such "jellybacks" and cowards, and afraid to be "a mouth of brass, a mouth of prophecy, and brazened-faced" for Yehovah's Holiness. How much judgment will be endured before Yahweh's true witnesses cry aloud?

African American

Many people have stated over the years that the African Slave Trade consisted of the Tribes of Israel who were scattered after the Romans invaded Jerusalem in 70 A.D. DNA technology has been able to validate much of this to be true. Genetics does not lie and there are so many genetic companies today who have taken enough genetic samples from millions of people globally that pinpointing ancestry lines have become an amazing advancement. Many African Americans' DNA has been verified and we are not from the bloodline of Ham. In other words, we were captured in Africa and sold into slavery, but our origins are not from Ham (Ethiopia, Egyptian, Libyan, or Canaanite) but from Shem. Many of us are Semitic.

The Gospels record of the Jews inaccurately assumes that all the Tribes of Israel were present during the time of Yeshua on Earth. We know Yeshua and His parents (Joseph and Mary) were both from the Tribe of Judah and that John the Baptist and both his parents (Zachariah and Elizabeth) were from the Tribe of Levi. Most of Yeshua's disciples were from Galilee and that area is where the Tribe of Benjamin populated. During the split of the tribes where Israel became the southern and northern kingdom, the southern kingdom consisted of Judah, Benjamin, and Levi and these three tribes are the ones who occupied Israel when Christ walked the Earth. After the scattering of the Jews in 70 A.D., the Tribes of Judah and Levi escaped to Egypt like the Israelites have done many times before. The Tribes of Israel were mixed with Egyptian and other African tribes from the very beginning, and this is why

Black Wives Matter

Egypt has always been an obvious place to escape to because their roots are there, and their skin color has always blended in.

The scattered Tribes of Judah and Levi migrated through Egypt and over the years worked their way to Western African known as the Horn of Africa. The African tribes knew who they were and although they were all Black, the locals knew they were descendants of Shem, and not Ham. Many of the African tribes converted to Islam and it was these Muslim tribes who captured and sold the Israelite Tribes into slavery, selling the slaves to the European slave traders. Over time, many of the descendants of Judah and Levi did not retain the rich knowledge of their godly heritage, although some did. The ones who were sold during the African slave trade, of course, were stripped of their spiritual heritage along with their native language, customs, and culture. As European property, we were made to learn their language, religion, and customs. Since 1619, Yahweh's people of the Tribes of Judah and Levi have survived enslavement in the Dominican Republic, Haiti, Jamaica, Bahamas, Virgin Islands, and America. Each of the slave colonies established in the Caribbean are directly connected to the lost people of Yahweh. I believe many in the slave trade were directly connected to the tribe of Levi and the bloodline of Phinehas (Black, Nubian, Brazen-Face), and we are the descendants and are not only a part of the Melchizedek Priesthood in Yeshua (if you're born-again) but also blood descendants of Phinehas and the Levitical Priesthood. God made a covenant and vowed that Phinehas' seed would be

Priests forever. Many of us are the fulfillment of that covenant.

11

Bathsheba

Daughter of an Oath, Daughter of Seven, and Seventh Daughter

&

Makeda

Greatness and Beautiful One

And David comforted Bathsheba his wife, and went in unto her, and lay with her: and she bare a son, and he called his name Solomon: and the Lord loved him.
2 Samuel 12:24

It was a Black woman who birthed all the sons of Judah, and it was Judah's Black daughter-in-law, Tamar, who birthed Judah's son Zerah. The Royal Line of Judah proceeded from Zerah. As the Tribe of Judah finally produced David as its first king, it would only seem fit that David would marry a Black woman named Bathsheba and their union would produce Solomon, the wisest and richest king of Israel. Bathsheba's first husband, Uriah, (who David set up to be murdered while in battle), was a Black man because he was a Hittite. Hittites were the descendants of Heth, one of Canaan's sons (Genesis 10:15). 2 Samuel 11:3 informs us that Bathsheba's father is Eliam. When we look at 2 Samuel 23:34, we will discover what tribe Eliam is from.

Eliphelet the son of Ahasbai, the son of the Maachathite, Eliam the son of Ahithophel the Gilonite.

Bathsheba's father was the son of Ahithophel the Gilonite. Gilonites were a Canaanite tribe and were of the Judean town of Gilho. Gilonites were the Canaanite tribes who were not expelled completely from their land during the conquest of Joshua. The Hittites were a sub-tribe of the Gilhonites who had settled in Gilhon. Therefore, Bathsheba was a Hittite. Ahithophel, a counselor of King David, betrayed the king and sided with David's son, Absalom during Absalom's rebellion. Bathsheba was a Black woman married to a Black man (Uriah the Hittite) until David got Bathsheba pregnant and had Uriah murdered. Uriah was one of David's Mighty Men. He was loyal and faithful to David until the end. This great Black man, warrior, and husband was righteous and honorable unto death.

Yahweh even remembers him in Yeshua's lineage. Matthew 1:6 says:

And Jesse begat David the king; and David the king begat Solomon of her that had been the wife of Urias (Uriah).

The judgment for the adultery and murder that David committed was the death of the son he had out of wedlock with Bathsheba. David's psalm of repentance for his sins and remorse for the loss of his son is recorded in Psalms 51:1-17. Afterwards, he married Bathsheba, and they had Solomon. However, Solomon was not the only offspring of David and Bathsheba. 1 Chronicles 3:5 lists three more sons from their union.

Solomon's Black Wives

Solomon was the wisest and richest king of Israel. Therefore, he reaped great benefits and one of these benefits was attracting the most powerful and beautiful women in the world. Solomon was the original "Player" and since "proper pimping" takes "preparation," this Black king established international trade routes, and brought peace to Israel on all sides. Solomon was one of the most unique men in all of human history and powerful women from every corner of the world sought him out. Solomon built the most expensive Temple that has ever been built. It was called the Temple of Solomon. It took seven years to build the Temple, but Solomon spent thirteen years building his own house. Why would his house take longer to build than Yahweh's house?

The answer is because Solomon had 700 wives and 300 concubines. Often, my pastor would say that there are three "G's" every man must avoid in order to keep from falling: Gold, Girls, and Glory. Solomon had all three, so he was a "Triple OG!" With great gifts, comes great responsibility. Solomon held it down for awhile but the accumulation of many foreign "dime-pieces,". . . I mean women, would be this Black man's downfall.

The Bride of Christ

Solomon's children from his 1,000 wives would all be Hebrew and Black because they came from the wisest and richest king of Israel who was Hebrew and Black. Ultimately, Solomon's marriage to so many wives of every ethnicity and race is a prophetic picture of the True King of kings and the One Who gave Solomon His riches and wisdom: Yeshua, Whose Bride consists of peoples of all kindreds, tribes, and tongues of the earth.

Pharaoh's Daughter

And Solomon made affinity with Pharaoh king of Egypt, and took Pharaoh's daughter, and brought her into the city of David, until he had made an end of building his own house, and the house of the LORD, and the wall of Jerusalem round about. 1 Kings 3:1

Pharaoh's daughters did not usually marry outside of their own family. As a descendant of Egyptian slavery, Solomon was changing the game when he married Pharaoh's daughter, revealing how Elohim exalted Israel from slavery to possessing the richest and wisest king alive. This famous Black king married this Egyptian, African princess.

Queen of Sheba

And when the queen of Sheba heard of the fame of Solomon, she came to prove Solomon with hard questions at Jerusalem, with a very great company, and camels that bare spices, and gold in abundance, and precious stones: and when she was come to Solomon, she communed with him of all that was in her heart.

And Solomon told her all her questions: and there was nothing hid from Solomon which he told her not.

And when the queen of Sheba had seen the wisdom of Solomon, and the house that he had built,

And the meat of his table, and the sitting of his servants, and the attendance of his ministers, and their apparel; his cupbearers also, and their apparel; and his ascent by which he went up into the house of the LORD; there was no more spirit in her. 2 Chronicles 9:1-4

The way to a woman's heart is through her ears. The serpent revealed this in the Garden of Eden as he successfully engaged her in conversation until he was able to beguile her into disobeying the commandment of Adonai. The Queen of Sheba's name is Makeda, and the land of Sheba was a royal city in the Ethiopian state.[60] We know Ethiopia was the name of Ham's firstborn son, Cush (Ethiopia). Sheba was actually the name of one of Cushs' grandsons. Genesis 10:7 reads:

And the sons of Cush; Seba, and Havilah, and Sabtah, and Raamah, and Sabtecha: and the sons of Raamah; Sheba, and Dedan.

Word of Solomon's wisdom reached the borders of Ethiopia and this powerful Black Queen of Sheba brought caravans of wealth to present to this extraordinary Black King of Israel. King Solomon operated in the spirit of excellence and that absolutely took Makeda's breath away. When Solomon's wives and concubines heard the Queen of Sheba was on her way to Jerusalem, they all got nervous. Then, when she arrived with camels loaded with gold, spices, and precious stones, Queen Makeda changed the game. She gifted Solomon with more wealth than any other kingdom. 1 Kings 10:10 records:

And she gave the king an hundred and twenty talents of gold, and of spices very great store, and precious stones: there came no more such abundance of spices as these which the queen of Sheba gave to king Solomon.

We talk about what a perspective spouse brings to the table. Well, Makeda brought her own table and plenty under the table. Yeshua spoke of Queen Makeda in His rebuke of the Jews who rejected Him as Messiah.

The queen of the south shall rise up in the judgment with this generation, and shall condemn it: for she came from the uttermost parts of the earth to hear the wisdom of Solomon; and behold, a greater than Solomon is here. Matthew 12:42

Makeda knew how many wives Solomon had, and she showed up to take over. Solomon gave Makeda his undivided attention and answered every question in her heart. This is one of the most attractive qualities any woman could ask of her man: the ability to listen and to answer the questions intelligently and compassionately in her heart. Solomon not only married Makeda, but she was the only wife who he built a throne for, and he placed it next to his throne. Queen Makeda became pregnant by Solomon and at six months pregnant decided to go back to her country. In the end, she understood she held the trump card. It could be stated that she broke Solomon. He was absolutely in love with Makeda and did not want her to leave. With the addition of conceiving his child, Makeda did what she came there to do like only Yahweh's Black women can; she rocked his world!

The Chronicles of Ethiopia record that upon Makeda's departure, Solomon (knowing she might be carrying his firstborn son), gave her his royal signet which would prove the child's bloodline. Makeda returned to Ethiopia and gave birth to Solomon's firstborn son and named him Menelik. At the age of eighteen, Menelik journeyed to Israel to meet his father, Solomon. When he entered the king's court, the servants could not believe how stunningly identical Menelik was to King Solomon. Menelik presented Solomon's royal signet and instantly, trouble began to rumor throughout the kingdom because people thought Menelik returned to claim his rightful position as the next King of Israel. Solomon's firstborn son (by an Israelite) threatened a civil war if Menelik claimed his firstborn status to the throne. However, Menelik only desired to meet his world-famous father. When Menelik departed to return home, King Solomon sent with him great gifts, and 1,000 people from each Tribe of Israel along with the Ark of the Covenant. Menelik became the first leader of the Solomonic Dynasty, and it is believed that the Ark of the Covenant is still in the protected custody of Ethiopian Hebrews today.[61]

12

The Mother of Rufus

Salute Rufus chosen in the Lord, and his mother and mine. Romans 16:13

The Holy Scriptures are full of unsung heroes. Many of Yehovah's most distinguished and exceptional vessels' names are not even mentioned. However, it does not mean the light of Yahweh's love was any less in these vessels than those who we are most familiar with in Scripture. The mother of Rufus is one of these noteworthy characters. The story of this precious woman of God, who Apostle Paul salutes in his epistle to the church at Rome begins with her husband who is another amazing hero. His story has not been properly told by our spiritual leaders today. His name is Simon.

Simon of Cyrene

And as they led him away, they laid hold upon one Simon, a Cyrenian, coming out of the country, and on him they laid the cross, that he might bear it after Jesus. Luke 23:26

Many have not realized how Yeshua had help on His journey to die for the sins of the world. In the Garden of Gethsemane, Yeshua's soul was in agony unto death and Father sent an angel to strengthen Him (Luke 22:42-44). Carrying the sins of the whole world was no small task that even Yeshua needed help carrying the Cross and who else understands the weight and plight of humanity better than Yahweh's first man, the black man? Simon was from Cyrene and Cyrene was a city in the African country of Libya. In the movie, *The Greatest Story Ever Told*, Sidney Poitier portrayed Simon of Cyrene. This was one of the very few times that Hollywood portrayed a biblical story, correctly. Simon of Cyrene is the husband of the mother of Rufus who Paul affectionately salutes in Romans 16:13. Mark 15:21 says:

And they compel one Simon a Cyrenian, who passed by, coming out of the country, the father of Alexander and Rufus, to bear his cross.

Simon was the father of Alexander and Rufus, the same Rufus Paul mentioned in the book of Romans. If Simon was from the African country of Libya, what was he doing in Jerusalem during Israel's high holiday of Passover? Acts 2:5-11 explains:

And there were dwelling in Jerusalem Jews, devout men, out of every nation under heaven.

Now when this was noised abroad, the multitude came together, and were confounded, because that every man heard them speak in his own language.

And they were all amazed and marvelled, saying one to another, Behold, are not all these which speak Galilaeans?

And how hear we every man in our own tongue, wherein we were born?

Parthians, and Medes, and Elamites, and the dwellers in Mesopotamia, and in Judaea, and Cappadocia, in Pontus, and Asia,

Phrygia, and Pamphylia, in Egypt, and in the parts of Libya about Cyrene, and strangers of Rome, Jews and proselytes,

Cretes and Arabians, we do hear them speak in our tongues the wonderful works of God.

Fifty days after the celebration of Passover was another high holiday called Pentecost and this passage reveals that devout Jewish men out of every nation were present. Why were they present? Because Yahweh's chosen people had been scattered throughout the earth many times over and during the times of Jesus, many made their pilgrimage back to Jerusalem for the high holidays that Yahweh instructed them to celebrate. Among the many nations listed, "Libya about Cyrene," was one of them and this is exactly where Simon, the husband of the mother of Rufus was from. This is why Simon of Cyrene was in Jerusalem during Passover and happened to be nearby during the crucifixion of Jesus. He was one of those devout Jews making his pilgrimage to the Holy Land. Simon was not just an African traveling to Jerusalem to celebrate Passover. He was of the bloodline of Israel.

It is quite possible that Simon did not know exactly Who Yeshua was. He was probably drawn to the crowd, wondering what was going on as the Son of God was being whipped with a cat-o'-nine-tails and wearing a purple robe. Maybe Simon had not heard that the Messiah had come and had no understanding of the weight of the moment he had stumbled upon. Nonetheless, in God's Sovereignty, Simon was handpicked to assist Christ in carrying the Cross. In essence, there was an echo throughout eternity; Yahweh chose and called the Black man to His side in His greatest time of need. Black men know what it is to be demonized, dehumanized, and downtrodden. He understands rejection, ridicule, and how it feels to be riled. Few places in Scripture are as poetic and prophetic, as this scene of Simon helping the Son of God to carry the Cross.

Imagine being Simon, thrust into such a sad and chaotic scene. He did not volunteer to carry the Cross. Simon was compelled to carry the Cross. We can imagine that once he realized that he had no choice in the matter, Simon finally positioned himself to bear the brunt of the weight of the Cross and as he was able to look upon Yeshua's brutally battered and bloodied body, he saw the unfathomable love of Yehovah. Though weakened and abused, the heart of Yahweh was on full display. Somehow through all the horror, Simon realized that he was in the Presence of his Creator and Yahweh's peace captured his soul. Many of the Scriptures concerning the coming Messiah's suffering must have flooded Simon's mind and Yehovah's Spirit gave him a revelation of what was occurring. At some point, Simon's assignment was completed, and he walked away in a daze. He later discovered that the Man Who's Cross he was forced to help carry was actually his long-awaited Messiah. I do not believe we can sufficiently relate to the overwhelming emotions that must have overcome Simon. We can only imagine how Simon told the story to his beloved wife and sons that the Scriptures were being fulfilled.

Maybe it wasn't until the Day of Pentecost that Simon's eyes were opened as he was one of the many who witnessed the one hundred and twenty followers of Christ speaking in the crowd's native languages, glorifying Yahweh, and Peter standing boldly before them explaining how Yeshua had come and died for the sins of the world. In this moment, Simon connected the dots and understood that it was His Savior

Who's Cross he was belabored with. There were 3,000 souls saved after Peter's exhortation and I believe Simon of Cyrene was one of them. No one among that Pentecostal group was touched quite like Simon because no one among them got close enough to touch Yeshua during His Passion. No other knew the true weight of the Cross and had such an intimate portrait of the price that our sins cost. Simon means *hearing, hearkening,* and *obeying*. Upon hearing Peter's anointed message on the Day of Pentecost, Simon hearkened and obeyed. The story of Simon of Cyrene is one for the ages and it is time we tell it.

Simon – Simeon

The names Simon and Simeon are actually interchangeable. They are variations of the same name and have the same meaning as Mary and Miriam. Acts 13:1 informs us:

Now there were in the church that was at Antioch certain prophets and teachers; as Barnabas, and Simeon that was called Niger, and Lucius of Cyrene . . .

Acts 11:19-20 says:

Now they which were scattered abroad upon the persecution that arose about Stephen travelled as far as Phenice, and Cyprus, and Antioch, preaching the word to none but unto the Jews only.

And some of them were men of Cyprus and Cyrene, which, when they were come to Antioch, spake unto the Grecians, preaching the LORD Jesus.

Believers who were scattered from Jerusalem because of persecution fled to Antioch and they were joined by Believers from Cyprus and Cyrene. One of the leaders of the Church at Antioch was a man named Simeon (Simon) from Cyrene, who was called "Niger." This was no doubt the same Simon of Cyrene who helped Yeshua carry His Cross. Simon went from carrying the Son of God's Cross on Passover to hearing the story of salvation by Peter on the Day of Pentecost. He graduated from simply being a blood Israelite, washed in the Blood of the Messiah as a new creation in Christ, to one of the leaders of the Church at Antioch. His promotion and respect were signified in his title, "Niger." This name is actually pronounced the way many say, "nigger," in a derogatory way. Yet, this was a term of endearment and respect given to one of Antioch's most beloved leaders. *Niger* means *Black* and he most definitely was not disrespected for his skin color but given the highest honor as a blood relative in the family of Israel and the one honored by Yahweh to help Yeshua carry the Cross. With the utmost honor, members of the Church at Antioch saluted this extraordinary man of God with the title "Niger." If you were close friends of Simon, you probably said, "My Niger." But this just goes to show you how contaminated certain words became over time, intentionally. African Americans use the term "nigger" with the same endearment as they did in the book of Acts. Simon was a leader and prophet at the Antioch Church and one of the leaders filled with the

Holy Ghost who fasted and prayed when Yahweh's Spirit said, *"Separate me Barnabas and Saul for the work whereunto I have called them."* Acts 13:2

Paul was taken to Simon's house after Barnabas brought him from Tarsus. By the time Paul wrote the epistle of Romans, it was thirty years after his conversion. Simon of Cyrene, the father of Alexander and Rufus, passed away (and probably Alexander also) at the time of Paul's salutation to Rufus and his mother. Paul called the wife of Simon of Cyrene, "your mother and mine." Paul's affection for this wonderful unnamed mother of Rufus ran deep. She not only received Apostle Paul into her home, but she also assisted him in many seasons of great distress. She was a mother to Apostle Paul spiritually and naturally as she cared for his many physical wounds and spiritual scars. She was a servant of Yahweh, a godly woman, and a mother who used her gifts of mercy and hospitality to minister to the citizens of the Kingdom of God. Her greatest asset was that she was a nurturer and loved her children as she reared them in the fear of Yehovah. She understood that her highest call was knowing her Father. There is no greater legacy than molding the next generation to be used by Yahweh. Paul called her son, Rufus, chosen in the Lord. What a wonderful family of Yahweh.

African mothers of God's chosen people are the true unsung heroes. They are never in the limelight but always on the heart of Yehovah. Sometimes they are not mentioned by name on the earth, but ever spoken before the Father in Heaven. Civilization was birthed by her, and all Hebrew bloodlines came through her precious womb. We are forever indebted to her and not enough has been stated concerning her pride, endurance, and extraordinary character. The creation of man was Yahweh's greatest creation. However, when He made woman – the second addition is always better than the first and she is the crescendo in the song of mankind's creation. Thank you, my African Queens.

Valediction

The purpose of this writing is to reveal the irrefutable biblical evidence of how Yahweh used His African women to birth every tribe in the Hebrew bloodline. As we come into greater understanding concerning the lost Tribes of Israel and Black people, we cannot forget that our salvation is not based on human DNA but the DNA of Yeshua. Yeshua became sin that we might be made the righteousness of Yahweh in Him (2 Corinthians 5:21). The truth needs to be heralded concerning Black people in Scripture, particularly, Yahweh's chosen people, Israel. Yehovah has a purpose and plan for the bloodline of true Israelites. However, salvation is only found in Christ Jesus our Lord, Yeshua Hamashiach. Yeshua said in John 8:31-32, *"If ye continue in my word, then are ye my disciples indeed. And ye shall know the truth, and the truth shall make you free."* The uniqueness of African Americans is how we are doubly blessed. First, we are connected to the natural bloodline of Israel. Second, we are connected to Israel spiritually, through the Blood of Yeshua. Maybe this is why the enemy fights us so hard. He wants to keep us from the amazing richness and royalty found in our heritage, both naturally and spiritually. As Apostle Paul affirmed in Romans

9:1-8, we are not children of Yahweh based on fallen human bloodlines, but we are made children of the Most High through the Atonement by the Precious Blood of Yeshua.

Prayer

Heavenly Father, I come to you admitting that I am a sinner. I choose to turn away from sin, and I ask You to cleanse me of all unrighteousness. I believe your Son Jesus, died so that I may be forgiven of my sins and made righteous through faith in Him. He took my place on the Cross so that I could take His place at your right Hand. I call upon the Name of Jesus Christ to be my Savior and the Lord of my life. I choose to follow You and I ask that You fill me with the power of the Holy Spirit. I declare I am a child of God. I am forgiven of my sins and full of the righteousness of God. I am saved. In Jesus' Name. **Amen.**

Footnotes

¹*Adam* means *man*. *Adam* is H120 in the Strong's Concordance and is the Hebrew word *adam* from H119 (meaning red) and it means ruddy for example a human being (an individual or the species, mankind, etc.):- another, hypocrite, common sort, low, man (mean, of low degree), person.
https://www.blueletterbible.org/lexicon/h120/kjv/wlc/0-1/; ©2022 Blue Letter Bible; Accessed on 10/13/22.

²*Living* is H2416 in the Strong's Concordance and is the Hebrew word *hay* or *chay* from H2421 (meaning to live): alive; hence, raw (flesh); fresh (plant, water, year), strong; also (as noun, especially in the feminine singular and masculine plural) life (or living thing), whether literally or figuratively:— age, alive, appetite, (wild) beast, company, congregation, life(-time), live(-ly), living (creature, thing), maintenance, merry, multitude, (be) old, quick, raw, running, springing, and troop.
https://www.blueletterbible.org/lexicon/h2416/kjv/wlc/0-1/; ©2022 Blue Letter Bible; Accessed on 10/13/22.

Soul is H5315 in the Strong's Concordance and is the Hebrew word *nepes* or *nephesh* from H5314 (meaning to breathe) properly, a breathing creature, for example animal of (abstractly) vitality; used very widely in a literal, accommodated or figurative sense (bodily or mental):—any, appetite, beast, body, breath, creature, dead(-ly), desire, (dis-) contented, fish, ghost, greedy, he, heart(-y), (hath, jeopardy of) life (in jeopardy), lust, man, me, mind, mortally, one, own, person, pleasure, (her-, him-, my-, thy-) self, them (your) -selves, slay, soul, tablet, they, thing, (she) will, and would have it.
https://www.blueletterbible.org/lexicon/h5315/kjv/wlc/0-1/ ; ©2022 Blue Letter Bible; Accessed on 10/13/22.

³Definition of the word *answer*. Merriam-Webster definition #1a
1a: something spoken or written in reply to a question
https://www.merriam-webster.com/dictionary/answer ; Accessed on 10/13/22.

[4] Definition of the word *key*. Websters 1828 Dictionary definition #7:
That which serves to explain any thing difficult to be understood.
https://webstersdictionary1828.com/Dictionary/key ; Accessed on 10/13/22.

[5] McCray, Reverend Dr. Walter Arthur ; *The Black Presence in the Bible*; Black Light Fellowship Publishing ©January 1, 1995; page 20.

[6] *Ham* is H2526 in the Strong's Concordance and is the Hebrew word *Ham* or *Cham*. *Ham* means the same as the root word H2525 (meaning hot); hot (from the tropical habitat); Cham, a son of Noah; also (as a patronymic) his descendants or their country:—Ham.
https://www.blueletterbible.org/lexicon/h2526/kjv/wlc/0-1/ ;
©2022 Blue Letter Bible; Accessed on 10/13/22.

[7] *Cush* is translated *Ethiopia*. *Cush* is H3568 in the Strong's Concordance and is the Hebrew word *Kuwsh*: probably of foreign origin; Cush (or Ethiopia), the name of a son of Ham, and of his territory; also of an Israelite:—Chush, Cush, and Ethiopia.
https://www.blueletterbible.org/lexicon/h3568/kjv/wlc/0-1/ ;
©2022 Blue Letter Bible; Accessed on 10/13/22.

[8] *Mizraim* is translated *Egypt*. *Mizraim* is H4714 in the Strong's Concordance and is the Hebrew word *Mitsrayim* dual of H4693 (meaning the proper name, of a territory); Mitsrajim, for example Upper and Lower Egypt:—Egypt, Egyptians, Mizraim.
https://www.blueletterbible.org/lexicon/h4714/kjv/wlc/0-1/ ;
©2022 Blue Letter Bible; Accessed on 10/13/22.

[9] *Phut* is translated *Libya*. *Phut* is H6316 in the Strong's Concordance and is the Hebrew word *Puwt*; of foreign origin; Put, a son of Ham, also the name of his descendants or their region, and of a Persian tribe:—Phut, and Put.

https://www.blueletterbible.org/lexicon/h6316/kjv/wlc/0-1/ ; ©2022 Blue Letter Bible; Accessed on 10/13/22.

Phut is translated *Libya*. According to the Brown-Driver-Briggs Lexicon, Strong's H6316 is the proper name, of a people probably Libyans, or Libyan tribe; usually named with African peoples. https://www.blueletterbible.org/lexicon/h6316/kjv/wlc/0-1/ ; ©2022 Blue Letter Bible; Accessed on 10/13/22.

[10] *Canaan Land* is the *Holy Land* or *Israel*. Exodus 6:4 says, "And I have also established my covenant with them, to give them the land of Canaan, the land of their pilgrimage, wherein they were strangers." And Ezekiel 17:8 says, "And I will give unto thee, and to thy seed after thee, the land wherein thou art a stranger, all the land of Canaan, for an everlasting possession; and I will be their God." https://www.biblegateway.com (Put Exodus 6:4 & Ezekiel 17:8 in the search engine); ©2022 Blue Letter Bible; Accessed on 10/15/22.

[11] *Cush* means *burnt, fire like,* and *dark-skinned*. *Cush* is H3568 in the Strong's Concordance and is the Hebrew word *Kuwsh*, probably of foreign origin; Cush (or Ethiopia), the name of a son of Ham, and of his territory; also of an Israelite:— Chush, Cush, Ethiopia. *Cush* = "*black*". https://www.blueletterbible.org/lexicon/h3568/kjv/wlc/0-1/ ; ©2022 Blue Letter Bible; Accessed on 10/15/22.

[12] *Chaldeans* is another name for *Babylonians*. Ezekiel 12:13 My net also will I spread upon him, and he shall be taken in my snare: and I will bring him to Babylon to the land of the Chaldeans; yet shall he not see it, though he shall die there. www.Biblegateway.com (Put Ezekiel 12:13 in the search engine); Bible Gateway, a division of The Zondervan Corporation, 3900 Sparks Drive SE, Grand Rapids, MI 49546 USA; Accessed on 9/28/22.

[13] *Abram* means *great father*. *Abram* is H87 in the Strong's Concordance and is the Hebrew word *Abram* contracted from

H48; high father; Abram, the original name of Abraham:—Abram. https://www.blueletterbible.org/lexicon/h87/kjv/wlc/0-1/ ; ©2022 Blue Letter Bible; Accessed on 10/15/22.

Abraham means *father of many nations*. *Abram* is H85 in the Strong's Concordance and is the Hebrew word *Abraham* contracted from H1 and an unused root (probably meaning to be populous); father of a multitude; Abraham, the later name of Abram:—Abraham. https://www.blueletterbible.org/lexicon/h85/kjv/wlc/0-1/ ; ©2022 Blue Letter Bible; Accessed on 10/15/22.

[14]*Ham's n*ame means *black, hot, swarthy* and *dark-skinned*. *Ham* is H2526 in the Strong's Concordance and is the Hebrew word *Ham* or *Cham* and means the same as the root word H2525 (meaning hot); hot (from the tropical habitat); Cham, a son of Noah; also (as a patronymic) his descendants or their country:—Ham. https://www.blueletterbible.org/lexicon/h2526/kjv/wlc/0-1/ ; ©2022 Blue Letter Bible; Accessed on 10/15/22.

[15]*Hagar* is H1904 in the Strong's Concordance and is the Hebrew word *Hagar* of uncertain (perhaps foreign) derivation; Hagar, the mother of Ishmael:-Hagar. https://www.blueletterbible.org/lexicon/h1904/kjv/wlc/0-1/ ; ©2022 Blue Letter Bible; Accessed on 10/15/22.

[16]Pareles, Jon: *U2, India Arie and Alicia Keys Lead Grammy Nominations;* https://www.u2station.com/news/2002/01/u2-india-arie-and-alicia-keys-lead-grammy-nominations.php#gsc.tab=0 ; Copyright © 2002 The New York Times Company. All rights reserved. Accessed on 9/28/22.

44th Annual Grammy Awards by Wikipedia; https://en.wikipedia.org/wiki/44th_annual_grammy_awards (Put 44th annual grammy awards in the search engine and click on the first article); Wikipedia® is a registered trademark of the Wikimedia Foundation, Inc., a non-profit organization. Accessed on 9/28/22.

¹⁷*Isaac* means *laughter*. *Isaac* is H3327 in the Strong's Concordance and is the Hebrew word *Yitschaq* from H6711; laughter (i.e. mockery); Jitschak (or Isaac), son of Abraham:—Isaac. Compare H3446.
https://www.blueletterbible.org/lexicon/h3327/kjv/wlc/0-1/ ;
©2022 Blue Letter Bible; Accessed on 10/16/22.

¹⁸*Keturah* means *incense, fragrant smoke, perfume* and *aloe-wood*. *Keturah* is H6989 in the Strong's Concordance and is the Hebrew word *Qetuwrah*; feminine passive participle of H6999; perfumed; Keturah, a wife of Abraham:—Keturah.
https://www.blueletterbible.org/lexicon/h6989/kjv/wlc/0-1/ ;
©2022 Blue Letter Bible; Accessed on 10/16/22.

H6999 in the Strong's Concordance is the Hebrew word *Qatar*, a primitive root (identical with through the idea of fumigation in a close place and perhaps thus driving out the occupants); to smoke, for example turn into fragrance by fire (especially as an act of worship):—burn (incense, sacrifice) (upon), (altar for) incense, kindle, and offer (incense, a sacrifice).
https://www.blueletterbible.org/lexicon/h6999/kjv/wlc/0-1/ ;
©2022 Blue Letter Bible; Accessed on 10/16/22.

¹⁹ *Ishmael* means *whom God hears*. *Ishmael* is H3458 in the Strong's Concordance and is the Hebrew word *Yishmael* from H8085 and H410; God will hear; Jishmael, the name of Abraham's oldest son, and of five Israelites:—Ishmael.
https://www.blueletterbible.org/lexicon/h3458/kjv/wlc/0-1/ ;
©2022 Blue Letter Bible; Accessed on 10/16/22.

²⁰*Per* in Latin means through, during, by means of, on account of, as in," from PIE root **per-** (1) "forward," hence "through, in front of, before, first, chief, toward, near, around, and against.
https://www.etymonline.com/word/per- ; © 2001-2022 Douglas Harper; Accessed on 9/29/22.

Fume in Latin from Latin fumus smoke, steam, fume, old flavor" (source also of Italian *fumo*, Spanish *humo*), from PIE root **dheu-** (1) "dust, vapor, and smoke.

https://www.etymonline.com/search?q=fume ; © 2001-2022 Douglas Harper; Accessed on 9/29/22.

[21]Definition of perfumery: 1a: the art or process of making perfume
b: the products made by a perfumer
2: an establishment where perfumes are made
Merriam-Webster Dictionary online https://www.merriam-webster.com/dictionary/perfumery
© 2022 Merriam-Webster, Incorporated; Accessed on 9/11/22.

[22]Powered by The archaeologist; *The 3200 Year Old Perfume of Tapputi, the First Female Chemist in History, Came to Life Again*; July, 2022
https://www.thearchaeologist.org/blog/the-3200-year-old-perfume-of-tapputi-the-first-female-chemist-in-history-came-to-life-again ; Accessed on 9/11/22.

[23]*Judith* means *praise Yehovah*. Judith is H3067 in the Strong's Concordance and is the Hebrew word *Yehuwdiyth;* the same as H3066; Jewess; Jehudith, a Canaanitess:—Judith. H3066 Y^ehûwdîyth is the feminine of H3064 Y^ehûwdîy. Y^ehûwdîy is patronymically from H3063 *Yehuwdah* which is from H3034. H3034 in the Strong's Concordance is the Hebrew word yadah; a primitive root; used only as denominative from H3027; literally, to use (for example hold out) the hand; physically, to throw (a stone, an arrow) at or away; especially to revere or worship (with extended hands); intensively, to bemoan (by wringing the hands):—cast (out), (make) confess(-ion), praise, shoot, and (give) thank(-ful, -s, -sgiving).
https://www.blueletterbible.org/lexicon/h3067/kjv/wlc/0-1/ ; Accessed on 10/16/22 and
https://www.blueletterbible.org/lexicon/h3034/kjv/wlc/0-1/ ; ©2022 Blue Letter Bible; Accessed on 10/16/22.

[24]*Bashemath* means *spice,* and *fragrance. Bashemath* is H1315 in the Strong's Concordance and is the Hebrew word *Bosmath;* feminine of H1314 (the second form); fragrance;

Bosmath, the name of a wife of Esau, and of a daughter of Solomon:—Bashemath, Basmath. H1314 in the Strong's Concordance is the Hebrew word *Besem* or בֹּשֶׂם *bôsem*; from the same as H1313; fragrance; by implication, spicery; also the balsam plant:—smell, spice, sweet (odour).
https://www.blueletterbible.org/lexicon/h1315/kjv/wlc/0-1/ ; Accessed on 10/16/22 and
https://www.blueletterbible.org/lexicon/h1314/kjv/wlc/0-1/ ;
©2022 Blue Letter Bible; Accessed on 10/16/22.

[25]*Adah* means *beauty, comeliness, adornment, ornament,* and *pleasure*. Adah is H5711 in the Strong's Concordance and is the Hebrew word *Adah*; from H5710; ornament; Adah, the name of two women:—Adah.
https://www.blueletterbible.org/lexicon/h5711/kjv/wlc/0-1/ ;
©2022 Blue Letter Bible; Accessed on 10/16/22.

[26]*Aholibamah* means *tent of the high place*. Aholibamah is H173 in the Strong's Concordance and is the Hebrew word *Oholiybamah*; from H168 and H1116; tent of (the) height; Oholibamah, a wife of Esau:—Aholibamah.
https://www.blueletterbible.org/lexicon/h173/kjv/wlc/0-1/ ;
©2022 Blue Letter Bible; Accessed on 10/16/22.

[27]*Mahalath* means *beautifully adorned, mild, smooth, pleasing to the touch, rhythmic movements, sweet,* and *harmonious sounds*. Mahalath is H4258 in the Strong's Concordance and is the Hebrew word *Machalath*; the same as H4257;sickness; Machalath, the name of an Ishmaelitess and of an Israelitess:—Mahalath. *Mahalath = stringed instrument*.
https://www.blueletterbible.org/lexicon/h4258/kjv/wlc/0-1/ ;
©2022 Blue Letter Bible; Accessed on 10/16/22.

[28]*Hirah* means *pure, noble, highborn, splendid, distinguished, freedom,* and *liberty*. Hirah is H2437 in the Strong's Concordance and is the Hebrew word *Chiyrah* from H2357 in the sense of splendor; Chirah, an Adullamite:—Hirah. *Hirah = a noble family*.
https://www.blueletterbible.org/lexicon/h2437/kjv/wlc/0-1/ ;
©2022 Blue Letter Bible; Accessed on 10/16/22.

²⁹*Adullamite* means *justice of the people, and equity of the people.*
Adullamite is H5726 in the Strong's Concordance and is the Hebrew word *Adullamiy*; patrial from H5725; an Adullamite or native of Adullam:—Adullamite. *Adullamite = see Adullam justice of the people;*
https://www.blueletterbible.org/lexicon/h5726/kjv/wlc/0-1/ ;
©2022 Blue Letter Bible; Accessed on 10/16/22.

³⁰*Shuah* means *a sinking down (as in the mud), settling down, bowed down (the mind or soul), despair, depressed,* and *pit.*
Shuah is H7744 in the Strong's Concordance and is the Hebrew word *Shuwach*; from H7743; dell; Shuach, a son of Abraham:—Shuah. *Shuah = wealth;*
https://www.blueletterbible.org/lexicon/h7744/kjv/wlc/0-1/ ;
©2022 Blue Letter Bible; Accessed on 10/16/22.

³¹*Er* means *awake, watchful, alert,* and *watchman.* Er is H6147 in the Strong's Concordance and is the Hebrew word *Er*; from H5782;
watchful; Er, the name of two Israelites:—Er. *Er = awake.*
https://www.blueletterbible.org/lexicon/h6147/kjv/wlc/0-1/ ;
©2022 Blue Letter Bible; Accessed on 10/16/22.

³²*Judah* means *praise.* Judah is H3063 in the Strong's Concordance and is the Hebrew word *Yehuwdah* from H3034; celebrated; *Jehudah (or Judah),* the name of five Israelites; also of the tribe descended from the first, and of its territory:—Judah. H3034 is the Hebrew word *yadah;* a primitive root; used only as denominative from H3027; literally, to use (for example hold out) the hand; physically, to throw (a stone, an arrow) at or away; especially to revere or worship (with extended hands); intensively, to bemoan (by wringing the hands):—cast (out), (make) confess(-ion), praise, shoot, and (give) thank(-ful, -s, -sgiving).
https://www.blueletterbible.org/lexicon/h3063/kjv/wlc/0-1/ ;
Accessed on 10/16/22 and
https://www.blueletterbible.org/lexicon/h3034/kjv/wlc/0-1/
©2022 Blue Letter Bible; Accessed on 10/16/22.

³³*Onan* means *able bodied, strong, stout, virile,* and *vigorous. Onan* is H209 in the Strong's Concordance and is the Hebrew word Ownan; a variation of H207; strong; Onan, a son of Judah:—Onan.
https://www.blueletterbible.org/lexicon/h209/kjv/wlc/0-1/ ; Accessed on 10/16/22.

³⁴*Tamar* means *palm tree, upright, standing forth,* and *ascending. Tamar* is H8559 in the Strong's Concordance and is the Hebrew word Tamar; the same as H8558; Tamar, the name of three women and a place:—Tamar.
H8558 is the Hebrew word tamar; from an unused root meaning to be erect; a palm tree:—palm (tree).
https://www.blueletterbible.org/lexicon/h8559/kjv/wlc/0-1/ ; Accessed on 10/16/22 and
https://www.blueletterbible.org/lexicon/h8558/kjv/wlc/0-1/ ; ©2022 Blue Letter Bible; Accessed on 10/16/22.

³⁵*Ibid.*

³⁶McCray, Reverend Dr. Walter Arthur; *The Black Presence in the Bible*; Black Light Fellowship Publishing ©January 1, 1995; pages 126-128.

³⁷Ginzberg, Louis *The Legends of the Jews* online; Legends of the Jews 2:1:74 Reuben's wife was named **Elyoram**, the daughter of the Canaanite Uzzi of Timnah. Simon married his sister Dinah first, and then a second wife. *The Legends of the Jews* by Louis Ginzberg [1909]; **Volume II: Bible Times and Characters from Joseph to the Exodus;** *The Wives of the Sons of Jacob – paragraph 3*;
https://www.friendsofsabbath.org/home ; (Type in the Search engine: Reuben's wife was named Elyoram); Click on **The Legends of the Jews: Volume II - Joseph;** Accessed on 9/30/22.

³⁸Ginzberg, Louis *The Legends of the Jews* online; Legends of the Jews 2:1:77 Asher's first wife was Adon, the daughter of Ephlal, a grandson of Ishmael. She died childless, and he

married a second wife, Hadorah, a daughter of Abimael, the grandson of Shem. *The Legends of the Jews* by Louis Ginzberg [1909]; **Volume II: Bible Times and Characters from Joseph to the Exodus;** *The Wives of the Sons of Jacob* – paragraph 6; https://www.friendsofsabbath.org/home ; (Type in the Search engine: Asher's first wife was Adon); Click on **The Legends of the Jews: Volume II – Joseph;** Accessed on 9/30/22.

[39]Ginzberg, Louis *The Legends of the Jews* online; Legends of the Jews 2:1:78 Zebulon's wife was Maroshah, the daughter of Molad, a grandson of Midian, the son of Abraham by Keturah. *The Legends of the Jews* by Louis Ginzberg [1909]; **Volume II: Bible Times and Characters from Joseph to the Exodus;** *The Wives of the Sons of Jacob* – paragraph 6; https://www.friendsofsabbath.org/home ; (Type in the Search engine: Zebulon's wife was Maroshah); Click on **The Legends of the Jews: Volume II – Joseph;** Accessed on 9/30/22.

[40]Ginzberg, Louis *The Legends of the Jews* online; Legends of the Jews 2:1:79 For Benjamin, when he was but ten years old, Jacob took Mahlia to wife, the daughter of Aram, the grandson of Terah, and she bore him five sons. At the age of eighteen he married a second wife, Arbat, the daughter of Zimran, a son of Abraham by Keturah, and by her also he had five sons. *The Legends of the Jews* by Louis Ginzberg [1909]; **Volume II: Bible Times and Characters from Joseph to the Exodus;** *The Wives of the Sons of Jacob* – paragraph 6; https://www.friendsofsabbath.org/home ; (Type in the Search engine: For Benjamin, when he was but ten years old); Click on **The Legends of the Jews: Volume II – Joseph;** Accessed on 9/30/22.

[41]*The Book of Jasher* **online; CHAPTER 45--*An Account of the Families of Jacob's Sons*;** Chapter 45:1 And it was at that time in that year, which is the year of Joseph's going down to Egypt after his brothers had sold him, that Reuben the son of

Jacob went to Timnah and took unto him for a wife Eliuram, the daughter of Avi the Canaanite, and he came to her. https://sacred-texts.com/chr/apo/jasher/45.htm ; Accessed on 10/16/22.

[42] ***The Book of Jasher** online; CHAPTER 45--An Account of the Families of Jacob's Sons.* Chapter 45:19-20 And Zebulun went to Midian, and took for a wife Merishah the daughter of Molad, the son of Abida, the son of Midian, and brought her to the land of Canaan. And Merushah bare unto Zebulun Sered, Elon and Yachleel; three sons. https://sacred-texts.com/chr/apo/jasher/45.htm ; Accessed on 10/16/22.

[43] *Mixed, ereb,* means *mingled, woof (woven fabric)* and *interwoven. Mixed* is H6154 in the Strong's Concordance and is the Hebrew word *ereb;* (1 Kings 10:15), (with the article prefix), from H6148; the web (or transverse threads of cloth); also a mixture, (or mongrel race):—Arabia, mingled people, mixed (multitude), woof. https://www.blueletterbible.org/lexicon/h6154/kjv/wlc/0-1/ ; ©2022 Blue Letter Bible; Accessed on 10/16/22.

[44] *Asenath* or *Asnat* means *dedicated to Neith. Asenath* is H621 in the Strong's Concordance and is the Hebrew word Acenath; of Egyptian derivation; Asenath, the wife of Joseph:—Asenath. https://www.blueletterbible.org/lexicon/h621/kjv/wlc/0-1/ ; ©2022 Blue Letter Bible; Accessed on 10/16/22.

Asenath or *Asnat* means *dedicated to Neith.* According to the Brown-Driver-Briggs Lexicon, Strong's H621 is the proper name, feminine wife of Joseph; Egyptian, = belonging to (goddess) Neith (Thes.) Cook; https://www.blueletterbible.org/lexicon/h621/kjv/wlc/0-1/ ; ©2022 Blue Letter Bible; Accessed on 10/16/22.

[45] Wikipedia; *Neith;* Neith is a borrowing of the Demotic form Ancient Egyptian: *nt,* likely originally to have been nrt "she is the terrifying one"; Coptic: also spelled Nit, Net,

or Neit was an early ancient Egyptian deity. She was said to be the first and the prime creator, who created the universe and all it contains, and that she governs how it functions. She was the goddess of the cosmos, fate, wisdom, water, rivers, mothers, childbirth, hunting, weaving, and war. https://en.wikipedia.org/wiki/neith; Paragraph 1; Wikipedia® is a registered trademark of the Wikimedia Foundation, Inc., a non-profit organization. Accessed on 9/28/22.

[46]US Census Bureau; *Black Demographics, The African American Population*; June 2022; First graph under: *2021 Black Population in US breakdown;* https://blackdemographics.com/population/ ; Source: U.S. Census Bureau, Population Division; Accessed on 10/16/22.

[47]Jeffrey, Terence P.; *Abortion Disproportionately Targets Black Babies; CDC: 74% of Abortions in Mississippi Were Performed on Black Mothers*; CNS News online article was written on May 24, 2022; Excerpt from paragraph 10: Table 6 of the CDC report presents the "[n]umber of reported abortions, by known race/ethnicity and reporting area of occurrence." It shows that 94.5 percent of the abortions—or 345,929 abortions—that occurred in 2019 in the 29 states and the District of Columbia that reported their abortions by race/ethnicity to CDC were in fact reported to the CDC. **Of this total of 345,929 abortions, 132,878 (or 38.4 percent) were performed on black mothers.** Another 115,486 (or 33.4 percent) were performed on white mothers; 72,509 (or 21.0 percent) were performed on Hispanic mothers; and 25,056 (or 7.2 percent) were performed on mothers of another race/ethnicity. https://cnsnews.com/article/national/terence-p-jeffrey/abortion-disproportionately-targets-black-babies-cdc-74 ; Copyright 1998-2022 CNSNews.com; CNSNews.com is a division of the Media Research Center; Accessed on 9/30/22.

[48]Longbons, Tessa; *More African-American Babies are Aborted Than Born Alive in New York City*; Article written on December 21, 2018. Excerpt from paragraph 3: A little over half of the women getting abortion in New York City – 56 percent – were

between the ages of 20 and 29. Nine percent were under the age of 20, 31 percent were in their thirties, and four percent were age 40 or older. **Non-Hispanic black women made up the largest group of women who obtained abortions in New York City, accounting for 39 percent of reported abortions.** Hispanic women made up the second-largest racial category at 28 percent of abortions, and white women made up 15 percent of the abortions reported in the city. Three-quarters of the women were unmarried. Fifteen percent were married, and 10 percent did not report their marital status. Ninety-three percent of the abortions reported in New York City were performed on city residents. https://www.lifenews.com/2018/12/21/more-african-american-babies-are-aborted-than-born-alive-in-new-york-city/ ; LifeNews.com; COPYRIGHT © 2003-2022; ALL RIGHTS RESERVED; Accessed on 9/30/22.

[49] *Shiphrah* means *bright, shining, splendid, polished,* and *beautiful. Shiphrah* is H8236 in the Strong's Concordance and is the Hebrew word *Shiprah*; the same as H8235; Shiphrah, an Israelitess:—Shiphrah. https://www.blueletterbible.org/lexicon/h8236/kjv/wlc/0-1/ ; ©2022 Blue Letter Bible; Accessed on 10/16/22.

H8235 is the Hebrew word *Shiphrah* from H8231; brightness:— garnish. https://www.blueletterbible.org/lexicon/h8235/kjv/wlc/0-1/ ; ©2022 Blue Letter Bible; Accessed on 10/16/22.

And H8231 is the Hebrew word *shaphar*; a primitive root; to glisten, i.e. (figuratively) be (causatively, make) fair:— goodly. To be pleasing, be beautiful, be fair, be comely, be bright, glisten; (Qal) to be beautiful. https://www.blueletterbible.org/lexicon/h8231/kjv/wlc/0-1/ ; ©2022 Blue Letter Bible; Accessed on 10/16/22.

[50] *Puah* means *mouth, orifice, blast, utterance,* and *command.* Puah is H6326 in the Strong's Concordance and is the Hebrew word *Puwah*; from an unused root meaning to glitter; brilliancy; Puah, an Israelitess:—Puah.
https://www.blueletterbible.org/lexicon/h6326/kjv/wlc/0-1/ ;
©2022 Blue Letter Bible; Accessed on 10/16/22.

According to the Gesenius' Hebrew-Chaldee Lexicon, *Puah* means *mouth* and *splendid.*
https://www.blueletterbible.org/lexicon/h6326/kjv/wlc/0-1/ ;
©2022 Blue Letter Bible; Accessed on 10/16/22.

[51] *Reuel* means *friend of God, shepherd of God,* and *led of God.* Reuel is H7467 in the Strong's Concordance and is the Hebrew word Reuwel; from the same as H7466 and H410; friend of God; Reuel, the name of Moses' father-in-law, also of an Edomite and an Israelite:—Raguel, Reuel.
https://www.blueletterbible.org/lexicon/h7467/kjv/wlc/0-1/ ;
©2022 Blue Letter Bible; Accessed on 10/16/22.

[52] *Jethro* means *His abundance, His superiority,* and *His excellence.* Jethro is H3503 in the Strong's Concordance and is the Hebrew word *Yithrow*; from H3499 with pron. suffix; his excellence; Jethro, Moses' father-in-law:—Jethro. Compare H3500. *Jethro = his abundance.*
https://www.blueletterbible.org/lexicon/h3503/kjv/wlc/0-1/ ;
©2022 Blue Letter Bible; Accessed on 10/16/22.

H3499 in the Strong's Concordance is the Hebrew word *Yether* from H3498; properly, an overhanging, for example (by implication) an excess, superiority, remainder; also a small rope (as hanging free):— abundant, cord, exceeding, excellancy(-ent), what they leave, that hath left, plentifully, remnant, residue, rest, string, and with.
https://www.blueletterbible.org/lexicon/h3499/kjv/wlc/0-1/ ;
©2022 Blue Letter Bible; Accessed on 10/16/22.

[53] *Hobab* means *beloved, cherished,* and *comforted.* Hobab is H2246 in the Strong's Concordance and is the Hebrew word *Chobab*; from H2245; cherished; Chobab, father-in-law of Moses:—Hobab. https://www.blueletterbible.org/lexicon/h2246/kjv/wlc/0-1/ ; ©2022 Blue Letter Bible; Accessed on 10/16/22.

H2245 in the Strong's Concordance is the Hebrew word *chabab*; a primitive root (compare H2244, H2247); properly, to hide (as in the bosom), for example to cherish (with affection):—love.
https://www.blueletterbible.org/lexicon/h2245/kjv/wlc/0-1/ ; ©2022 Blue Letter Bible; Accessed on 10/16/22.

[54] *Putiel* which means *afflicted of God. Putiel* is H6317 in the Strong's Concordance and is the Hebrew word *Puwtiyel*; from an unused root (probably meaning to disparage) and H410; contempt of God; Putiel, an Israelite:—Putiel. *Putiel = afflicted of God.*
https://www.blueletterbible.org/lexicon/h6317/kjv/wlc/0-1/ ; ©2022 Blue Letter Bible; Accessed on 10/16/22.

[55] Bar-Am, Aviva and Shmuel; *Israel's Druze honor the prophet Jethro in annual pilgrimage to ancient tomb*; April 24, 2018 https://www.timesofisrael.com/israels-druze-honor-the-prophet-jethro-in-annual-pilgrimage-to-ancient-tomb/ ; © 2022 THE TIMES OF ISRAEL, All Rights Reserved; Accessed on 10/17/22.

[56] Hobab which means *beloved, cherished,* and *comforted* is today's Black man. Hobab is H2246 in the Strong's Concordance and is the Hebrew word *Chobab*; from H2245; cherished; Chobab, father-in-law of Moses:—Hobab.
https://www.blueletterbible.org/lexicon/h2246/kjv/wlc/0-1/ ; ©2022 Blue Letter Bible; Accessed on 10/17/22.

[57] Abarim Publications, *The names of MALE characters in the Bible;*

The Name Phinehas: Summary; BDB Theological Dictionary suggests that it is a transliteration of the Egyptian name *Penehasi*, meaning The Negro, or more specifically, The Bronze-Colored One, says HAW Theological Wordbook of the Old Testament; https://www.abarim-publications.com/NaLi/A-MaleBig.html ; (Scroll down to "P" and click on Phinehas); Go to *Etymology and Meaning of the Name Phinehas*; paragraph 1; ©Abarim Publications; TXu1-364-624; Accessed on 10/17/22.

[58]The name "Phinehas" probably comes from the Egyptian name Panehasi, Panehesy (Coptic: ⲡⲁⲛⲉϩⲁⲥ). According to the *Oxford Companion to the Bible*, "the Bible also uses Egyptian and Nubian names for the land and its people ... For the Egyptians used to these color variations, the term for their southern neighbors was Neḥesi, 'southerner', which eventually also came to mean 'the black' or 'the Nubian'. This Egyptian root (nḥsj, with the preformative p˒ as a definite article) appears in Exodus 6.25 as the personal name of Aaron's grandson, Phinehas (= *Pa-neḥas*)"; Under Name; 1st paragraph; https://en.wikipedia.org/wiki/phinehas ;Wikipedia® is a registered trademark of the Wikimedia Foundation, Inc., a non-profit organization; Accessed on 10/17/22.

[59]The Hebrew meaning of *Phinehas* is *mouth of prophecy, mouth of brass, brazened faced,* and *bold-unabashed*. *Phinehas* is H6372 in the Strong's Concordance and is the Hebrew word *Piynechac*; apparently from H6310 and a variation of H5175; mouth of a serpent; Pinechas, the name of three Israelites:—Phinehas. Phinehas = "mouth of brass." https://www.blueletterbible.org/lexicon/h6372/kjv/wlc/0-1/ ; ©2022 Blue Letter Bible; Accessed on 10/17/22.

[60]Sauter, Megan, *Who Is The Queen of Sheba in the Bible? Investigating the Queen of Sheba and Her Kingdom*; September 6, 2022; paragraph 4; Dated between the 6th–14th centuries C.E., the *Kebra Nagast* (*The Glory of Kings*) is an important text to the Ethiopian Orthodox Church. It names **the Queen of Sheba as the beautiful queen Makeda and**

identifies the land of Sheba as ancient Ethiopia. Kribus thoroughly examines the latter claim in his article "Where Is the Land of Sheba—Arabia or Africa?"; Biblical Archaeology Society online; © 2021 Biblical Archaeology Society; https://www.biblicalarchaeology.org/daily/ancient-cultures/ancient-near-eastern-world/who-is-the-queen-of-sheba-in-the-bible/ ; Accessed 10/17/22.

[61]Black History in the Bible; *King Menelik I, The Solomonic Dynasty, and The Ark of The Covenant*; March 23, 2018; Paragraphs 1,2 & 3 under *Menelik I and The Ark of The Covenant;* https://www.blackhistoryinthebible.com/research-studies/king-menelik-i-the-solomonic-dynasty-and-the-ark-of-the-covenant/ ; Accessed on 10/17/22.

Pastor Romel Duane Moore Sr. can be 808-371-0597.

Website is www.romelduanemooresr.com

Made in the USA
Columbia, SC
27 November 2022